THE
LEADERSHIP
CONSTANT

Also by Dr. Judy Morley

5 Spiritual Steps to Overcome Adversity

THE
LEADERSHIP
CONSTANT

AUDACIOUS STRATEGIES FOR NAVIGATING CHANGE

DR. JUDY MORLEY

MEDIA

MEDIA

Published 2022 by Gildan Media LLC
aka G&D Media
www.GandDmedia.com

FIRST EDITION 2022

Front cover design by David Rheinhardt of Pyrographx

Interior design by Meghan Day Healey of Story Horse, LLC

Library of Congress Cataloging-in-Publication Data is available upon request

ISBN: 978-1-7225-0598-1

10   9   8   7   6   5   4   3   2   1

Contents

1

Rethinking Transitions

Change is inevitable, except from a vending machine.
—ROBERT GALLAGHER

Greek philosopher Heraclitus's famous statement about change being the only constant is as true today as it was 2,500 years ago. This may not be good news for most people. Humans have been conditioned to dread, fear, and avoid changes. Throughout human history, however, changes have always brought benefits. No growth, evolution, or advancement happens without change. The evolution of social structures, businesses, governments, and institutions throughout the millennia show that change has, indeed, been constant. Moreover, change has been the driving factor behind all progress.

Change itself is neither inherently good or bad. All things are in flux—whether the rapidly multiplying cells of the body, changing seasons, shifting weather, or trending cultural movements. Everything is either growing or dying. All technological, cultural, and intellectual advancements stem from a constant energetic flow of change.

As prevalent as change is, human beings are inherently uncomfortable with it. For something so fundamental, it is paradoxical and yet axiomatic that people resist it. The reasons for resistance include biological, psychological, and cultural factors.

First, humans' biological makeup strives to maintain the status quo. To survive, bodies seek homeostasis, which is the state of remaining the same. On the macro level, homeostasis gives the illusion of inertia. However, it is not the absence of change, but actually thousands of tiny changes happening so rapidly that they appear to be unmoving. Regardless of what's happening beneath the surface, all appearances point to business as usual.

Additionally, human brains are wired to prefer repetitive tasks. The basal ganglia, located in the most primitive parts of the brain, enable people to perform routine tasks with minimal energy. This survival mechanism is the reason you can push a grocery cart, talk on a cell phone, avoid other shoppers, and solve a problem at work while still breathing and blinking. The basal ganglia ingrain habits so that much of your life happens on autopilot. If you've ever driven home from work and not remembered doing it, you know what I mean. All this biological programming seems to keep us in a rut.

Psychological factors also contribute to the human resistance to change. Comfort zones create the situations, attitudes, and sometimes physical places that feel safe, familiar, and calming. Comfort zones are a way to make sense of changes in life, creating almost-mechanistic processes to get through day-to-day existence. Parents frequently create routines for children to help them feel secure, from brushing teeth to bath time to bedtime stories.

Once you grew up, you probably not only continued these routines, but you also created more. Whether you are driving to work the same way every day, doing chores, or figuring out relationships, your comfort zones provide the feeling of mastery over your environment. The familiarity is a cornerstone to mental health and a sense of well-being.

Third, cultural factors provide barriers to change. Although Americans claim to value innovation, most prefer the status quo. Culture changes slowly, and although each generation thinks they lead a cultural revolution, each so-called revolution is ultimately co-opted into the prevailing culture. No generation has a monopoly on either virtue or vice. Sexual promiscuity, violence, and the perception of decaying values are common to every era.

In the twentieth century, technological innovation masked the slow pace of cultural change. Penicillin, space travel, television, personal computers, and mobile phones gave the illusion of innovation, while racism, misogyny, xenophobia, and paternalism persisted. Lasting cultural innovations are rare. Conservative cultural forces rely on nostalgia for a past that never was, to slow the pace of cultural change.

Despite all these resistant factors, change happens. Sometimes humans instigate it, hoping for something better. More frequently, people are thrust into transitions against their will. Although the first kind of change seems like a welcome event, a long period of adjustment still occurs—almost a grieving process for the past that's been left behind. If a change comes quickly from an outside force, however, it feels frightening and overwhelming. It takes time to process the emotions and adapt to a new environment with a new set of rules.

Therapists advise against making major life decisions after a significant change, such as starting a different job, moving to a new home, or losing a loved one. They understand that change upsets the cognitive faculties and causes stress that leads to mistakes and poor judgment.

Leadership in a Changing Organization

As difficult as change is for individuals, the level of complexity is multiplied in organizations. Rapidly changing conditions provide specific challenges to leadership. If you have picked up this book, you are probably looking for a way to lead an organization, team, or community through a time of transition. Each individual within a company must go through their personal process of adapting to change, while structures and procedures must also be evaluated, modified, or overhauled.

As with people, organizational adaptation takes place whether the change is positive—such as occurs with an expansion or new product—or negative—like layoffs or a takeover. Organizational leaders must perform a particularly tricky juggling act to be empathetic to individuals adapting to the new circumstances while also creating new policies and procedures—even as they continue to do business as usual.

In his classic book *Good to Great*, author Jim Collins talks about the organizational tension brought on by changes. According to Collins, any time an innovation occurs, a company must balance between preserving core values and stimulating progress. Core values are the cornerstone of every business identity and need to be honored and preserved.

Progress, however, is the mechanism for growth and maintaining a competitive edge. Since progress entails change, it is easy for a business to avoid it. Good companies lean too heavily on either preservation or progress; *great* companies find the perfect balance between the two.

If individuals are hardwired to resist change, and organizations even more so, why does our friend Heraclitus say it is the only constant? Anyone who has lived to adulthood realizes that change happens all the time. Change is the primary mechanism for evolution, innovation, and progress.

If you asked a caterpillar while it was spinning its cocoon, it probably would not say it was excited about the upcoming transition. It is evolutionarily driven to encase itself in a fiber prison, completely dissolve, and then regrow, cell by cell, into what looks like a different animal. Yet the change created a thing of greater beauty. The caterpillar has no choice in the matter, and, really, from the perspective of living a fulfilling life, neither do you.

Change through Audacious Leadership

How do you lead—yourself and others—through the upheaval of change? One word: *audaciously*. Recently, *audacious* has become my favorite descriptor. The definition of audacity is "bold, daring, unique, unlimited." When changes come barreling ahead and every biological, psychological, and cultural system goes into red alert, it takes boldness and daring to meet and embrace it. Without audacity, there is no change, no progress, no growth. The conscious act of leading audaciously in the face of change is the difference between survival and failure—both for individuals and organizations.

In my years as a coach and speaker, clients come to me because they want their lives to be different. They want their businesses to be more successful, their relationships to be more fulfilling, their bodies to be healthier, and their friendships to be more authentic. In general, they want their lives to be more peaceful.

Yet when I ask what they are willing to *change* to get their desired result, they immediately lose their enthusiasm. I call this reaction the I-want-everything-to-be-different-but-nothing-to-change syndrome. Ironically, humans crave improvement but resist change. You can't have one without the other.

If you operate from the premise that the upheaval of transition has a lasting benefit, the next step is to see what, exactly, the benefit is. One of the greatest benefits of changing conditions is to remind and reconnect individuals and organizations with their purpose. Transitions provide an opportunity to reevaluate *why* you do what you do. When stripped of daily routines, conditioned behaviors, and outgrown procedures, people and companies are forced to reconnect with the passion that started them on the journey in the first place. It's no longer enough to just be efficient since systems and tasks easily fall away. The new environment demands greater creativity to accomplish big goals.

Big changes that seem negative generally end up being enormous benefits in the long run. Most people can relate to a challenging event—like a layoff, diagnosis, or divorce—turning into a huge blessing in the long run.

Years ago, I had a business that started with great promise. I was a consultant for developers of historic real estate. In my first year, I worked with multiple clients, plenty of contracts, and new leads coming from all directions. When the real estate market crashed in 2008, the need for my services crashed as well. My business failed, and I had to get a job—something that I thought I would never do again.

Within a year, however, the new job opened a new career path that reconnected me to my higher purpose. The job created opportunities I never imagined and gave me a platform to rebuild. Furthermore, every employee I had to lay off found new jobs that were a better fit for each of them, and all of us made more money. As painful as it was to close my business and get a job, the result was so much better than anything I could have orchestrated. When my greatest fear happened, the change reinforced my purpose and provided a benefit I never dreamed of.

Experiences like this sparked my fascination with leading through change. I have a PhD in history, and as a leader, the past inspires me to see how things can work better. By looking at change through the wide-angle lens of history, transitions clearly facilitate growth and progress. In historical circles, this is called (appropriately academically) evolutionary transformation. There is a sociological theory of change called the Hegelian dialectic. Despite the stuffy name, this theory provides a powerful description of how changes breed progress.

Named after the early-nineteenth-century German philosopher Georg Hegel, the Hegelian dialectic begins with a thesis, which is the current condition, the status quo, what *is*. Since change is a constant, however, all situations eventually elicit a reaction, which is frequently the opposite or anti-"thesis." The antithesis contradicts the thesis, causing intellectual and cognitive tension.

The only way to resolve the tension is to find a way to bridge the opposing sides, which leads to a syn-"thesis" of these ideas. The synthesis then becomes a new thesis, or status quo, and the evolutionary process begins again. From a historical perspective, all change is a factor of the ongoing dialectic process.

Why should you care about the abstract academic construct of the Hegelian dialectic? Because it provides uncanny accuracy to describe how things evolve. In organizations and personal lives, there is always the status quo—the thesis. Then someone gets an idea how to improve, and immediately there is a new goal that may or may not harmonize with the status quo—thus, the antithesis. The two ideas exist simultaneously until one of them ultimately gives way; a synthesis is created and becomes the new status quo, or thesis.

Here is a real-world example. Think about retail shopping. For centuries, as far back as the Middle Ages, buying things meant going to a store. Until the twenty-first century, the thesis was to drive to a location, wander around until you found what you needed, pay the merchant for it, and bring it home. Enter Amazon, the antithesis. From the comfort of your couch, you now order whatever you want and never get out of your jammies. Currently, a new synthesis is emerging, where you can shop online and pick it up in store or find what you want in a showroom and order it to be delivered. This is a perfect example of the Hegelian dialectic at work and how change drives evolution.

If all evolution comes from change, people must get over their resistance and learn to adapt. Leaders, especially, must become personally comfortable with change to move their followers through it. Leadership has many definitions, but they all include some version of influencing people to reach a desired outcome.

The Value of Practice

To reach a goal, a group or organization must inherently face changes. It takes audacious leadership to motivate people out of their natural preference for inertia and into a new level of excitement about making changes that they are programmed to resist.

- How do you effectively lead through change when you face the dazed, frightened, automatic reactions of your colleagues and followers, as well as yourself?

- How do you adjust your own attitude so you can lead your teams to be excited and motivated when everyone's first impulse is to hunker down and dig in?

The answer is practice. All skills take practice. For example, consider learning the piano. You could read every book ever written about the piano, understand the working of the instrument, study the great composers, learn to read music, and memorize famous concertos. None of this would help you when asked to sit at a keyboard for the first time and play a sonata. You must practice.

Similarly, you must practice adapting to change and getting out of your comfort zones, both in your own life and in your organization. Leaders help colleagues practice by emphasizing that goal setting, process evaluation, and other forms of innovation are not only encouraged but expected. You must continue to move people out of their comfort zones and into a cordial relationship with change. Like my mother hovering over my fourteen-year-old self at the family piano, you must encourage and enforce practice.

Of course, slow changes are easier to handle than rapid ones, but, either way, leaders must master navigating change and become proficient at motivating others to embrace it as well. Whether dealing with a welcome transition, such as a new strategic plan, an ambitious goal, or a life-altering decision, or a change that is unexpected, like fluctuating market conditions, a hostile merger, layoff, or global pandemic, remember that on the other side is the success, prosperity, happiness, and peace you desire. When you learn how to believe in this completely, you inspire those around you to get on board and ride the wave of change to a new, better destination.

As technology increases the pace of life, as communication travels faster than ever, and as information threatens to overwhelm at any moment, it is more important than ever to master change. Like the common *Serenity Prayer* by theologian Reinhold Niebuhr, you must have the serenity to accept the things you cannot change, the courage to change the things you can, and the wisdom to know the difference.

The more proficient you get at navigating change, the better equipped you are to lead others. Only then can you be a beneficial presence on the planet. Isn't that why most people choose to become leaders in the first place?

What We Can Learn from the Civil War

This book combines my two passions—audacious leadership and history. History provides excellent examples of audacious leadership strategies. Stripped of the politics of contemporary life, these historical situations give pure examples of audacious leadership, along with context and hindsight to analyze what worked and what did not. Audacious leadership is particularly valuable in rapidly changing, stressful environments.

Among the most studied historical events for leadership training is the American Civil War, particularly the Battle of Gettysburg. Considering I live in Gettysburg, I might be a little biased, but government agencies, Fortune 500 companies, and global leaders have come to Gettysburg for the past 150 years to study and understand what the battle and its aftermath say about leadership.

In the following chapters, I outline five audacious strategies, illustrated by examples from the Civil War, the Battle of Gettysburg, and contemporary businesses. Each strategy is considered audacious because it didn't necessarily follow the prescribed norms and called for bold, daring action. The success of these strategies in the microcosm of the Battle of Gettysburg is reinforced by a contemporary example in the macrocosm of today's business world. If the use of these strategies can change the course of humanity, they can certainly beef up your leadership.

In case you do not remember your history classes, the American Civil War took place from 1861 to 1865. It rocked the nation to its core. Although the disagreement about slavery and its expansion was present since the founding of the first colonies, the rapidity of westward expansion and industrialization in the early nineteenth century were flash points for issues that had been simmering for a century. When the issues finally came to a head, the change was fast and devastating.

In the midst of the Civil War, ordinary people were thrust into positions of leadership by necessity. Conditions changed so quickly that the need for leadership was overwhelming, and every situation seemed to be untested. The US Army on the eve of the Civil War was essentially a frontier constabulary with about 16,000 officers and men scattered around seventy-nine different posts. Within a matter of months, this organization grew to a force of 150,000 men. Who had the audacity to get them organized? Uniformed? Trained? Fed? There was no one with experience in these gargantuan leadership tasks.

Similarly, no doctors were prepared to treat the carnage that lay ahead. Pre–Civil War medicine was an individual thing, with doctors knowing their patients personally. Hospitals might be able to tend to five or ten patients at once, in the case of a fire or a flood, but 3,000 casualties, such as they had at the First Battle of Bull Run? Or 51,000 casualties at Gettysburg? No one was prepared for the magnitude of the task. Consequently, leaders had to come up with audacious solutions to unprecedented problems to bring about a synthesis of old and new.

What about feeding the troops? Most food was grown and distributed locally to relatively small communities. Suddenly, within thirty days, an army of close to 100,000 men descended on Washington, DC. Where would the Department of the Army get food? Who would cook it? How would they distribute it? These unprecedented questions demanded audacious answers.

How did leaders step forward and overcome these hurdles to evolve and solve new problems? They were forced to practice getting comfortable with change. It did not come naturally, but they learned it, nevertheless. They saw that the status quo was changing, and they broke through both personal and organizational resistance to create new structures and ultimately a new culture. It took planning, preparation, and personnel, but, most importantly, it took audacity.

Contemporary Applications for History's Lessons

Audacious leadership is a combination of personal growth, relationship savvy, and strategic vision-casting. Each chapter of this book includes an explanation of the strategy, a historical example to illustrate the strategy, and a contemporary example to show a broader application. The final pages of each chapter include tips to help you implement the strategy.

The historical examples that illustrate the points are episodes most people have heard of and can relate to. History provides the benefit of perspective to see the outcome and look at how change drove evolution and elevated humanity to a new reality. The contemporary examples show how these timeless strategies work in today's marketplace. Good leadership is timeless, and by tying a historical example to a contemporary one, it makes the strategies more understandable, relevant, and, most importantly, doable.

The strategies go from personal to organizational. The first audacious strategy for leading through change is to lean into it. In chapter 2, I discuss how to practice your own adaptability. I teach how to monitor your thoughts about change and reframe any negative thoughts or panic. I show the importance of rethinking the impact of past changes and learning how to look ahead to anticipate what might be on the horizon. This is part intuition, part emotional intelligence, and part skill practice.

I cite Abraham Lincoln, arguably the greatest president, and show how he befriended change starting as a boy. Throughout his life, he honed his emotional intelligence skills and listened to his intuition to issue one of the most progressive documents in the nation's history. I then discuss Vera Wang, who started her career thinking she would be a professional ice skater and ended up as a successful designer and entrepreneur. I close this chapter with practical exercises for you to learn how to lean into it.

In chapter 3, you will learn when to defy the odds, which means connecting with a purpose, reviewing your resources, watching competitors, finding the tipping point, and being proactive. Change is rarely a surprise, and by practicing this strategy, you can have a creative response to what's coming. To exemplify this, I cite the example of Union cavalry Brigadier General John Buford who had the audacity to face down four times his number of troops to effectively position his army. By taking a calculated risk, he made the difference between victory and defeat.

To bring this point to the present, I highlight Steve Jobs, who defied the odds in the computer industry and completely redefined how humans use technology. Again, at the end of the chapter are tips for you to practice knowing when to defy the odds.

In chapter 4, I illustrate how to do the unexpected. Human nature dictates reacting in well-rehearsed, predictable ways. Sometimes, however, the best strategy is to throw the rule book out the window and do the unexpected. For this tactic to be effective, however, leaders must take the time to gain the trust of their followers. Without a bedrock belief that situations will always work out for a greater good, it is almost impossible to embrace change. The trust necessary to do the unexpected comes from an alchemic combination of transparency, integrity, clarity, empathy, and inspiration.

For this illustration, I use Colonel Joshua Lawrence Chamberlin and his amazing example of building trust and getting people to do the unexpected at the Battle of Gettysburg. His startling response in a rapidly changing environment turned the tide of the battle and, consequently, the war. For a twenty-first-century example, I talk about Chip and Joanna Gaines, whose Magnolia empire is built completely on trust and continues to grow despite their personal choice to pull back. As in every chapter, there are practice prompts to get you ready to do the unexpected.

Chapter 5 tackles the difficult topic of knowing when to do nothing. Most people are trained to immediately swing into action to manage chaos. Since change is messy and fraught with risk, it is natural to do everything to avoid or stop or fix what is happening and try to reinstate the status quo. Frequently, however, you are most powerful when you do nothing.

I tell the story of Union General George Meade's anticipation of Pickett's Charge, a controversial risk and response at Gettysburg, in which doing nothing worked to lure Meade's opponents into making a fatal, fateful attack. More recently I use the example of the Malice in Dallas, where Stevens Aviation CEO Kurt Herwald and Southwest Airlines CEO Herb Kelleher decided to do nothing to settle a trademark dispute and both came out winners. The exercises at the end of this chapter help you identify how to know when doing nothing is your best bet.

In chapter 6, I describe how to act as if. Change is an opportunity to crack out of the shell of limitation and step into a greater reality. Humans create meaning by labeling events either good or bad. If you label a major change as something that will break you, you consequently stay broken. If, however, you learn to act as if a new, better reality is a foregone conclusion, you reframe your experience and see each transition as a passage between something that is ready to be left behind, and something that is ready to be embraced. I explain how to use the formula E+R=O to learn to intentionally define meaning and tell a new story.

I examine the Gettysburg Address, one of the greatest speeches of all time, and identify how it created an entirely new identity for the United States in just 272 words. For a contemporary example, I talk about Oprah Winfrey's decision to take her first ratings failure as the catalyst to build her media empire. As always, I provide you with practice techniques for acting as if.

As frightening as change can be, learning to handle it is the key to growth, success, and personal peace. No one inherently loves change. However, by practicing how to adapt, showing that you can survive it, and creating a relationship of respect and excitement around change, you can learn to weather the storms and move through them with grace and aplomb.

Each of these five audacious strategies serves to tie you back to your own audacious purpose. I am excited to guide you on this journey of resiliency, and to share with you examples of leadership in rapidly changing, stressful environments. I am confident that by the time you are finished with this book, you will have the audacity to befriend change!

2

Lean Into It

What we resist, persists.
—CARL JUNG

One of my mentors once told me, "You can't teach anyone something you haven't learned yourself." As obvious as this sounds, many people don't practice it. If you've ever tried to get a teenager to do something you won't do, you know what I mean. They'll point it out to you pretty quickly. You can learn the theory of something and teach it hypothetically, but without experience, it's impossible to have empathy for someone else's progress. This is especially true about guiding people through change. To lead others through turbulent times, you have to be comfortable with change yourself. This is the first audacious strategy: lean into it.

If you already have a wonderful relationship with change, seek it out, look for ways to shake up life, and are addicted to the adrenaline rush of a new experience, congratulations! You are definitely in the minority of humanity. I urge you to keep practicing, however. There are always ways to improve, and everyone can build a more insightful relationship with transitions.

If, however, you are like most people who prefer that everything stay the way it is, welcome to the club. Whether you learned to dread change from parents or authority figures, had your own catastrophic experiences, or have just avoided change for so long that you are completely unfamiliar with it, you must lean into it if you want to be an effective leader.

Leaning into it means being willing to embrace change when it comes, rather than pulling away from it, which is most people's natural tendency. It's a metaphor for the body language used when something is pleasant—you lean into it. When something is unpleasant, you tend to draw back. To be a leader through change, you must fight the impulse to draw back and, instead, lean into it.

Because human nature resists change, most initial reactions to an unexpected event are to back away, cling to the past, fight the tide, and do whatever possible to maintain the status quo. This inflexible attitude may feel comfortable in the moment—reverting to your comfort zones—but it can have disastrous long-term consequences. What happens to the rigid tree that stands against the wind, or the rock colliding with water? They break. Change is more jarring and violent to them than to the tree that bends or the sand that gives way.

Change is generally a gift wrapped in the trappings of adversity. Most people don't embrace change because they equate it with misfortune. Not all change, however, is negative, and as trite as it sounds, every seeming adversity holds the seed of opportunity.

If you were ever laid off a job, you probably viewed it at the time as a terrible challenge that evoked fear, worry, and rejection. Most likely, you found a new job that was more fulfilling, easier to do, and higher paying. Perhaps you took the opportunity to start a business or retire early. Most people who have been laid off say that, in the long run, it was the best thing that happened to them. Change forced them out of their comfort zone and gave them an immediate reason to pursue their dreams.

The same is true for a serious health challenge. Most cancer patients who survived five years said that cancer was the greatest gift they'd ever received. This is not because they are masochists. I am a twenty-plus-year cancer survivor, and this is certainly true for me. The experience made them reevaluate their lives, appreciate the things that they had taken for granted, and adapt their lives to find more pleasure and fulfillment.

To lean into change, you need a high degree of emotional intelligence. Unlike cognitive intelligence, or IQ, which is fixed at birth, emotional intelligence, or EQ, is a skill you can learn. Emotional intelligence is made up of four subordinate skills: self-awareness, self-management, social awareness, and relationship management. The first two subskills are how you handle yourself, and the second two are how you handle relationships. Self-awareness and self-management are the most valuable skills to help you lean into change. By honing these skills, transitions won't cause you upheaval, worry, or fear.

The foundation of strong EQ is mastering your own emotions. Start by building self-awareness. In general, people are not taught to recognize what they feel, when they feel it. As a matter of fact, you were probably taught the contrary. Well-meaning authority figures told you that your scraped knee didn't really hurt or that your bruised emotions were nothing to cry about.

To have strong self-awareness, you must overcome years of conditioning that taught you to disassociate from feelings. Learning to identify your feelings in the moment takes practice, but when you know what your feelings *really* are, not what you think they should be, you have achieved self-awareness.

You can help build self-awareness by paying attention to where in your body you feel emotions. Do you clench your jaw when you're angry? Ball up your fists? Does your stomach get queasy when you're sad? Do you blush when you're ashamed? Recognizing these clues helps you identify and understand your emotions, which prepares you to ride emotional waves without getting seasick.

Once your proficiency at self-awareness grows, the next step is to practice self-management. Self-management is critical for navigating stressful situations. Being frightened, angry, or stressed doesn't give you permission to take it out on those around you, whether family, friends, or colleagues. I call it "growing up" all over people, and it is a sign of low emotional intelligence. When you are faced with inordinate stress caused by a rapidly changing situation, self-awareness skills help you identify what you're feeling, then self-management skills allow you to choose appropriate reactions.

This is different from suppressing your emotions. Unexpressed emotions fester and build up until they create so much energetic pressure that they must explode. However, self-management allows you to consciously choose the most productive way to respond to a situation and modulate your behavior accordingly. Take deep breaths, go for a walk, or even meditate to calm down before interacting with people.

Sometimes the best way to practice self-management is to just be still. I love the quote from Henry David Thoreau: "Happiness is like a butterfly; the more you chase it, the more it will elude you, but if you turn your attention to other things, it will come and sit softly on your shoulder."

The same is true for peace, calm, or equanimity. You may not be calm about a changing situation immediately, but sit quietly for a few minutes, think about something else, and your emotions will come into check so that you are able to manage your reactions effectively.

Mastering personal emotional intelligence lays the groundwork for the first component of leaning into change, which is to monitor your mindset. As hard as it sounds, policing your thoughts and recognizing how each thought makes you feel allows you to consciously decide what to do rather than have knee-jerk reactions. The more frequently you successfully choose your behavior, the more confidence you have in your ability to handle change. When you give yourself credit for adapting and notice that you have improved how you handle change, you build trust in your abilities.

How, exactly, do you monitor your mindset? Stop and catch yourself when you think about transitional situations. What do you think of first? Do you dread the change? Criticize it? Do you let yourself get overly dramatic about situations that have simple solutions? Are you chronically asking why bad things always happen to you? If so, you have some negative habits you need to break.

My friend is a comedian. She offers improv classes to public speakers to teach them how to think on their feet. In her lessons, she forces every student to respond to each new exercise by clapping and saying, "Yay!" Frequently, the students are nervous about getting in front of the group and potentially looking foolish, so they generally don't feel enthusiastic. However, my friend makes them clap and cheer, regardless. She is forcing them to practice shifting their mindset.

She explains that when two comedians are doing a skit and one of them offers a lead-in to a scene, no matter how outrageous or unexpected, the only response can be, "Yay!" It isn't funny to watch actors quibble on stage about details. It isn't entertaining to have one comedian walk offstage in a huff because the other suggested that they do something embarrassing or ridiculous. The comedian must make the most out of the scene, no matter what. Whether out loud or mentally, the only response can be one of enthusiasm.

Although this exercise requires practice, this is exactly the mindset necessary to face changes. The next time your car breaks down, your job gets transferred to a different state, your relationship is in turmoil, the economy tanks, or your business is shut by a global pandemic, stop yourself before you get very far into throwing your pity party and clap your hands and say, "Yay!" Sure, it's natural to feel bad for a little while. It's a human process to grieve. But it's a skill set to bounce back. Practicing the skill makes it easier.

Shift your perspective to see that this is exactly the opportunity you've been looking for to get a new car, take an adventure, spend some quality time alone, reevaluate your investments, change careers, or laugh at the universe's sense of humor. As you practice this skill, you will stop taking everything as seriously, and so, in a self-fulfilling prophecy, the changes in your life won't seem as overwhelming or frightening. It takes practice, but monitoring your mindset is a habit well worth forming.

Second, take time to rethink how changes have impacted you in the past. Probably, the majority of changes you dreaded became great blessings with the benefit of hindsight. I remember the years I spent in an unhappy marriage, afraid to tell the truth to my spouse because I didn't want to hurt him. I also didn't want to give up my cozy lifestyle, with a nice car, large home, successful friends, steady paycheck.

Once I found the courage to say that I was unhappy, I thought the world would end. Yes, there were months of upheaval, divorce decisions, counseling with our small daughter, moving between houses and apartments, and plenty of heartache. Now, almost twenty years later, we are both much happier. He has been remarried for over fifteen years in a happy relationship that works for him. The same is true for me. Although the change was painful, the benefits were so much better than if we had continued to pretend to be happy. I'm certain you can think of similar examples from your own life.

Finding the silver lining in these past events makes it infinitely easier to face transitions in the present. Believe it or not, your attitude about the past changes everything that happens to you today. As crazy as it sounds, I did a transformational exercise years ago that completely reworked my relationship with time and memory.

My coach at the time had me rewrite my past. In my journal, I recounted my life story as if everything had happened exactly the way I would have wanted it.

I recounted my happy childhood, my loving family, my wealthy lifestyle, my happy romances, my perfect figure. Even though none of it was literally true, I wrote the story as if it were my best-selling autobiography. It was a fun exercise and provided a lot of peace.

The real magic happened the following month. Inexplicable coincidences occurred. My family became more understanding, money flowed easier, and my relationships all improved. I wasn't consciously trying to fix any of those things, but it was as if rewriting the past erased years of negative conditioning and transformed *me* into someone who had everything work out for her. I let go of my fear of change and reframed transitions as opportunities. This exercise proved to me that how you think about the past will transform your life today. Instead of being angry and upset about unpleasant past changes, this exercise brings closure, so your past doesn't continue to impact the present.

Third, practice anticipating changes. Look at every situation and ask the question, "What are the possible scenarios?" When you anticipate multiple situations, you can decide how to handle them if they materialize. Because building emotional intelligence is a skill that takes practice, it's beneficial to rehearse possible scenarios.

No one reacts well when caught off guard, but if you practice reacting to a variety of situations, you become adept at anticipating change. Of course, there are some changes no one can see coming—like a global pandemic—but, like all skills, anticipating change is transferable. Once you learn to understand your emotions and manage your reactions in changing environments, you can do it in *any* situation. Another benefit is you will start noticing changes in the early stages, rather than waiting until they happen and then being forced to be reactive.

Monitoring your mindset, rethinking the past, and anticipating the future all strengthen your emotional intelligence skills, which help you implement the audacious strategy of leaning into change. Why is it audacious? Because so few people can do it. Why is it important? Let's face it—team members don't feel inspired to embrace transitions when they watch their leaders freak out over little changes.

If you're running around like your hair is on fire, it's hard to inspire trust and confidence. Even if you are only freaking out on the inside, and you try to fake it by presenting an optimistic, confident demeanor about pending changes, your team members will smell a rat. You may fall apart later, but when leading your team, you must practice becoming truly calm in the face of change, and project that calm to those depending on your leadership.

Lessons from Honest Abe

Abraham Lincoln was a stellar example of leaning into change. Lincoln was not a religious man, but he was known to be introspective, spending much time brooding and contemplating deep issues. He also brilliantly controlled his emotions, particularly in public. While some historians claim that he suffered from "melancholy" or depression, which led him to withdraw from society, others portray him as a savvy leader who took the time to personally lean into change before leading the country through it.

His skill was the product of Lincoln's lifelong practice of getting comfortable with change. Although he adapted admirably to transitions throughout his life, the year 1862 was particularly difficult. The nation experienced setbacks on every front of the Civil War: a succession of failed commanders for the Union Army, a significant lost opportunity at the Battle of Antietam, and embarrassing defeats during the Peninsula Campaign, the Battle of Second Bull Run, and the Battle of Fredericksburg.

Lincoln felt the mounting casualty totals deeply and personally. On top of it all, his beloved son, Willie, died of typhoid fever that February, aged only eleven, which threw his wife, Mary Todd Lincoln, into a hysterical depression that lasted for months.

Multiple biographies illustrate that Lincoln spent the greater part of 1862 adapting to these changes and doing it alone. His ability to monitor his thinking about the changes, reframe past situations considering current circumstances, and anticipate what might come next gave him the clarity necessary to lead the country through the greatest crisis it faced. He modeled how to embrace change, rather than resist it, and showed the nation how to adapt with dignity and maturity.

Lincoln articulated his relationship with this stressful environment in a message to Congress in December 1862, a month before he signed the Emancipation Proclamation and seven months before the Battle of Gettysburg, the turning point of the war. In it, Lincoln revealed his thinking about the war, his ability to reframe the past, and a desire to anticipate what was next.

In his message, he told Congress, "The dogmas of the quiet past are inadequate to the stormy present. The occasion is piled high with difficulty, and we must rise with the occasion. As our case is new, so we must think anew, and act anew. We must disenthrall ourselves, and then we shall save our country."

That is leaning into change. Lincoln did not try to resist what was coming, but rather he embraced it. He admitted that the nation could not keep doing things the way it always had. He did not say that Congress should resist the changes, but rather that they must "rise with the occasion." He urged them to think and act anew and let go of attachments ("disenthrall ourselves") to the way things had always been done.

A Fashion Icon Embraces Change

One hundred and fifty years later, a very different person with a radically different experience used the same tools to lean into change. Entrepreneur and fashion designer Vera Wang experienced life-altering circumstances that might have caused her to give up, but, instead, she embraced them to become a leader in the world of both business and fashion.

Before she was a fashion icon, Wang trained as a figure skater. She began skating at age eight and became an Olympic hopeful in pairs skating. She competed in the 1968 US National Championships in Philadelphia. She was on her way to the 1968 Winter Olympics in Grenoble when she and her partner failed to qualify for the Olympic finals. Wang was devastated. That setback marked the end to her athletic career and completely changed the trajectory of her life. According to Wang, "I had a nervous breakdown and ended up doing a semester in Paris to recover."

While in Paris, Wang learned to lean into change. Rather than give up, she discovered a new passion for fashion, which helped her heal from the emotional blow of losing her skating career. She monitored her thinking about skating to develop a healthy relationship with the changes she experienced. She reframed the impact of her past and realized the experience was a stepping-stone to where she was meant to be.

Many of her early fashion designs were skating costumes. She anticipated upcoming changes and trends and incorporated them into her designs, making her a leader in the industry. By making peace with her past, she was able to design figure skating outfits for Olympians Nancy Kerrigan, Michelle Kwan, Evan Lysacek, and Nathan Chen. By leaning into change, Wang not only found a way to use it to her advantage but became a fashion leader and powerful business mogul.

To lean into change, you, too, must increase your emotional intelligence and do what it takes to embrace new situations. It is not enough to put a smiley face on and pretend that things are okay. You must find the wherewithal to think beyond the current circumstances and embrace the new reality, even if you can't yet see what that reality might be.

Exercises to Lean Into It

The following exercises will help you practice leaning into change. I recommend that you do them all, although you don't need to do them in any particular order. Grab a journal, set aside some quiet time, and begin to transform your relationship with change.

- Designate one day in which you don't complain about a single thing. Don't complain about changes at work, in the weather, with your family, or in politics. See if you can extend it to not complaining for a week. Try this practice for a month.

- If possible, take a different route to someplace you go daily. If you work in an office, go a different way to work. If you work from home, try varying your route to the grocery store. Try doing a different route every day for five days. Notice your reactions. Do you become irritated? Can you see the change as an adventure?

- Get a journal and rewrite your past. Write the past you would have loved to have had as if it really happened. Use your imagination and include as many details as possible.

- Take a day to practice saying "yay" to every situation you encounter. Have to take out the trash? Yay! Aren't you glad to have trash service? Get a speeding ticket? Yay! That cop may have saved your life. Fight with your spouse? Yay! It's an opportunity to make up.

- Choose a situation that, at the time, seemed like the change was a disaster. Journal about the situation. Can you find a silver lining to it? Can you find several?

- Look for potential changes on the horizon. Are market conditions fluctuating? Are you struggling with personnel shifts? Do you have aging family members? Take a few minutes to list as many possible future scenarios as you can.

3

Defy the Odds

When something is important enough,
you do it even if the odds are not in your favor.
—ELON MUSK

Once you have embraced a new relationship with change, you can move to the next strategy, which flies in the face of common sense: defy the odds. Typically, most people's reaction to change is to be cautious.

When faced with fear of the unknown, it seems reasonable to calculate the odds, evaluate options, and avoid risk. If your first impulse is to make the safest choice, that reaction is borne of fear, not foresight. Leading people in stressful times takes more than calculating odds and playing it safe. Sometimes, it takes audacity, and the most audacious strategy just might be to consciously defy the odds.

What does it mean to defy the odds? It means flouting convention, taking a risk, and following your gut instinct in the face of evidence to the contrary. Have you ever had a time when your intuition was telling you to do something illogical? Maybe you had a feeling to check your bank balance online. Something just didn't feel right. You probably thought of all the rational reasons why you shouldn't be fearful, but the nagging voice wouldn't stop. If you ignored it, you probably found out later that a forgotten charge went through and you were overdrawn. If you followed your gut, you defied the odds and probably saved yourself an overdraft fee.

Defying the odds doesn't mean being foolhardy or reckless. It means going through a process to assess the odds, determine your position, and do what's best to achieve your goal. Sometimes this happens below your level of awareness, and you decide so quickly you don't recall the process. It's a delicate balancing act between deliberation and audacity.

Five Ways to Defy the Odds

To use the strategy of defying the odds, first you must fully understand your current position. Start by reiterating your purpose. A strong purpose will always be your guide. Is it compelling? Is it appropriate? Is your team engaged with and excited by it?

When you find yourself amid change, it is imperative to have a well-defined, well-known purpose. A well-written purpose statement serves as the rubric to define your nonnegotiables and highlight where you are operating in congruence with that purpose and where you need to shift.

Second, check the status of your systems and resources. Is your structure set up to encourage your team to innovate, or are they stuck in an old, ineffective pattern? If you ask a team member why they do something and the response is, "Because that's how it's always been done," it signals outdated systems.

I'm reminded of the story of Grandma's Ham. One day, a husband read the newspaper in the kitchen while his wife prepared ham for dinner. The husband watched his wife cut about one inch off both ends of the ham. He asked why she did that, proclaiming, "That's a waste of good ham!"

She replied, "That's how my mom prepared it."

When her husband asked why her mom did it that way, the wife didn't know. Later, she called her mother to find out why she cut the ends off the ham, and her mom replied, "Because that was the way my mom prepared ham."

The wife's grandma had passed away several years earlier, but her grandpa was still living. She called him to ask why her grandma had cut the ends off the ham. He was silent for a moment, trying to recall, and then replied, "We were so poor when we got married that we only had a small pan, so she cut the ends off so that the ham would fit in the pan."

Obviously, using outdated systems is not a recipe for growth. Continuing to "cut off the ends of the ham" leads to stagnation and reduced efficiency. Such practices signal a lack of incentive to innovate and come up with new ideas. It is critical to audit systems for the right balance between stability and creativity. It can be tricky to find the balance between "if it ain't broke, don't fix it" and "innovate or die." Do you have the right people? The right methods? Is your team empowered to suggest changes when they see something wrong? Be sure to include upcoming, positive, planned initiatives in the resource inventory so you can prepare for multiple possible outcomes.

Third, look at your competitors. Have they done something different recently? If so, do you need to respond? Your response may not necessarily equate to making immediate changes, but it does mean that you must monitor the situation. Sometimes the changes made by your competitors are harbingers of bigger innovations happening in the industry, and sometimes they are major mistakes on the competitor's part, and you can watch the disaster unfold. Either way, be aware of your competitive surroundings. Know your odds for success before you try to defy them.

Toys R Us is an example of a company that miscalculated the odds. They incurred billions of dollars of debt to upgrade stores and expand inventory at a time when more and more toy shopping was being done online. Rather than identify a better strategy, Toys R Us reverted to doing what they had always done—just more of it. Instead of investing in a robust internet presence, the company "cut off the ends of the ham" by investing in their stores, and then couldn't make the payments on the billions of dollars of debt that weighed them down.

This major toy seller ignored their newest competitors, big box stores such as Target and Walmart, who were selling more toys than they were. They also miscalculated the power of online retailers like Amazon. Toys R Us took what they thought was a safe route that played to the odds, but they couldn't navigate the changes.

Fourth, look for a tipping point. In his significant book by that title, Malcolm Gladwell showed that there is generally a small event that causes big change. Gladwell starts the book by describing New York City in the 1970s. With murder and violent crime soaring out of control, new mayor Rudy Giuliani made a bold choice.

Realizing he couldn't tackle the astronomical violent crime rate overnight, the mayor decided to focus on what he could do, which included monitoring subway turnstiles for people who didn't pay, painting over graffiti, and fixing broken windows. These small changes prompted otherwise law-abiding citizens to care more about their environment. They began participating in the "policing" of their neighborhoods, and slowly the small changes in petty crime lowered the murder rate.

This phenomenon, also known as the broken window theory, is as true in organizational cultures as it is in the physical environment. What small change can you make that could have a major impact?

Fifth, be proactive. Look at the overall situation. Don't wait for conditions to surprise you and then react. Look at all possible scenarios and have contingency plans. For example, is the economy strong? Are new competitors entering the market? Do you have plans you can put into place if things change quickly? No one wants to expect the worst. As a matter of fact, I would be the first person to counsel against such a mindset. Expect the very best in your life and business. However, have a contingency plan in place in case something unexpected happens.

It's like a football team. No team goes into the game expecting to lose—they all start with a game plan to win. If they're getting their butts kicked by halftime, they switch out their game plan. Successful organizations anticipate possible disasters and are ready for them.

In his book *Good to Great*, author Jim Collins described the difference between being proactive and unrealistically optimistic. Frequently, leaders confuse the two. Collins identified the Stockdale Paradox, named for Admiral James Stockdale, the highest-ranking US POW during the Vietnam War. Tortured and imprisoned for eight years from 1965 to 1973, with no prisoners' rights and no guarantee of release, he organized and led the other POWs, keeping their morale up and giving them survival strategies in the "Hanoi Hilton."

Stockdale was brutally honest with his men about how bad things were. He told them the stark truth about their situation. In an interview, Collins asked Stockdale who was the least likely to survive as a POW. "The optimists," Stockdale replied, without skipping a beat.

His answer seemed counterintuitive to all that has been written about the power of positive thinking, but Stockdale was quite clear. "Oh, they were the ones who said, 'We're going to be out by Christmas.'

And Christmas would come, and Christmas would go. Then they'd say, 'We're going to be out by Easter.' And Easter would come, and Easter would go. And then Thanksgiving, and then it would be Christmas again. And they died of a broken heart ... This is a very important lesson. You must never confuse faith that you will prevail in the end—which you can never afford to lose—with the discipline to confront the most brutal facts of your current reality, whatever they might be."

When Collins asked Stockdale how he survived, he explained that, despite his devastating situation, he believed in the positive outcome. "I never lost faith in the end of the story. I never doubted not only that I would get out, but also that I would prevail in the end and turn the experience into the defining event of my life."

This attitude led Collins to identify the Stockdale Paradox: "Retain faith that you will prevail in the end, regardless of difficulties, and at the same time, confront the most brutal facts of your current reality, whatever they might be."

The Stockdale Paradox describes how to be proactive, even in a terrible situation. When you have faith that you will prevail, you are free to identify possible options. Proactive leaders don't rule out any opportunity, no matter how long a shot it seems. Sometimes, universal forces have a bigger picture than you can see in the moment. In these instances, it is your best bet to keep your options open and look for plans B, C, and D. No matter how focused you are on a result, market forces, different personalities, and unintended consequences can change the trajectory of your actions. Always look for a place to regroup and a back-up strategy in these instances.

Doing these five strategies—connecting with the purpose, evaluating your systems and resources, monitoring your competitors, watching for tipping points, and being proactive—will give you the information necessary to calculate the odds of success and make informed decisions. Sometimes the best course of action is to go with the odds. However, when things are changing quickly and a lot is at stake, sometimes the wisest strategy is to defy the odds.

Survey the Landscape

An instructive example of a leader who calculated the odds and then defied them was Brigadier General John Buford, Union cavalry general during the Battle of Gettysburg. In June 1863, Robert E. Lee and the Confederate Army invaded the North. They came looking for supplies, food, and a stunning victory that would both relieve the pressures of war on northern

Virginia and potentially bring the British into the Civil War as allies of the South. The Confederates entered southern Pennsylvania while the Union Army kept themselves between the rebels and Washington, DC.

On June 30, 1863, Buford got reports of Confederate lookouts a few miles west of a small crossroads in southern Pennsylvania called Gettysburg. In an odd turn of events, the Confederates approached from the north and the Union approached from the south. Buford took advantage of his march from Maryland into Pennsylvania to survey the landscape around him and develop a variety of strategic options. He mentally mapped out various places that would be beneficial in a battle and kept them in mind as he moved forward with his initial orders, which were merely to follow the Confederates, find out where they were, and *avoid a general engagement.*

The first thing Buford did was connect with his purpose. Buford's soldiers were the eyes and ears of the entire army. His purpose was twofold; to find the Confederates and to position the Union Army for success. That meant finding the right terrain, with elevated positions, access to supplies, and ease of troop movements. Buford knew his purpose was not to singlehandedly win the war or go for glory. He was to find the enemy and recommend the best place to fight them.

Buford assessed his resources and systems. He took stock of his troops, artillery, and ammunition. He had just under 3,000 men and realized he would be outnumbered by as much as ten times. He also knew that his cavalry carbines fired twice as fast as the Confederate muskets, so he picked up a bit of an advantage with weaponry. Additionally, his experience reminded him of a tactic he could use where he broke his cavalry into groups of four and dismounted them. One man would hold the horses while three fired. This tactic allowed Buford to maximize his system's efficiency, regardless of how many of the enemy he faced.

Buford also ascertained his resources by determining where the rest of his army was. He gauged how far away his commanding officer, General John Reynolds, was and how long his cavalry would have to hold the line before Reynolds's infantry arrived. He stayed in communication with Reynolds so he could manage his resources.

As the advanced guard, Buford kept tabs on his organization and gave them accurate information and good advice when they arrived on the field. Buford knew he had the trust of his commanding general, and he was confident in his decisions. Buford also had a strong grasp of the positions of the other Union commanders, how long it would take them to get to

Gettysburg, and their relative capabilities once they arrived. He knew which divisions would fight, which would run, and which would lag. Because Buford knew his organization, he was able to quickly come up with possible strategies to fight if the Confederates attacked.

And Buford had every reason to believe that the Confederates would attack. Because it was his job to know what his competitors were up to, he had reconnoitered the area and knew *exactly* who he was facing. There had been reports of Confederate soldiers across southern Pennsylvania, from Chambersburg to Harrisburg to York. Was Buford facing a small raiding party, one or two brigades, or the entire rebel army? The answer would obviously impact how and where Buford chose to engage them.

Instead of waiting to be surprised by their arrival, Buford sent out pickets and an advanced guard to reconnoiter the Confederates. He had comprehensive intelligence about which corps he faced, who the commanders were, the troop strength and position of the rest of the army. He knew that General Robert E. Lee's entire Army of Northern Virginia was spread out for close to sixty miles across southern Pennsylvania, and that *they* had no idea he was there. Buford's knowledge of the competition was so in-depth that, despite superficial appearances that the odds were against him, he felt confident that he could defy them and prevail.

Because Buford knew his competitors, he was able to find a way to tip the odds in his favor. In Buford's case, this tipping point was his route to Gettysburg. Unlike Lee, Buford had approached Gettysburg from the south, so he saw the creeks and hills that created tactically advantageous positions south of town. He realized that the series of parallel ridges provided him with ideal terrain to buy his army time. By attacking from the forward-most ridge, then falling back to the next ridge, called "defense in depth," he could stall the Confederates, who had to form new battle lines on each ridge. It was not much, but the advantage was enough.

Finally, Buford's actions were proactive. He asked townspeople who they had seen in town and checked newspapers to see where raiding had been reported. He put himself in the Confederate soldiers' shoes and anticipated what they would do. He relied on his experience of fighting the Confederate commanders in previous engagements. Buford knew their temperament and what they were likely to do. He laid out options and possible scenarios so he would be prepared to meet whatever was in front of him.

Buford didn't take these actions in a vacuum. When Buford reported back to General John Reynolds later that evening, he made sure to inform him of all the elements they faced. He knew his purpose was to find the exact position of the Confederate Army and stop, or at least delay, any rebel advance. He assessed his resources and systems and found his troops were well trained, well supplied, ready to fight, and in position. He knew his competition, having faced Lee's army on many other occasions, and was certain he knew what commanders were in front of him. He had taken the seemingly small step of noticing the terrain and identifying strong fallback positions. He took the proactive steps of planning alternate scenarios and notifying his commanding officer.

Because he had taken the time to adequately prepare and determine the odds, Buford knew that he could defy them. When the sun rose on July 1, 1863, Buford was on a series of ridges to the north and west of Gettysburg. He first saw the Confederates marching toward him from atop Herr's Ridge and began his delaying tactics. Because of all the information he had—about his staff, his systems, his competitors, the terrain, and the rest of his army—he quickly executed a plan.

Although he was dramatically outnumbered, he dismounted his men and harassed the Confederates as they came. He used geography to his advantage and relied on the rest of the First Corps of the Union Army to relieve them as fast as they could. Despite being outnumbered by 10,000 Confederates to his 2,500 troops, his in-depth knowledge and proactive planning assured him he could defy those odds.

General John Buford defied the odds to position the Union Army for success. Although he began the day on a rise west of town called Herr's Ridge, that was not Buford's ultimate desired position. He had written to General Reynolds that they wanted to keep the ultimate fallback position of Cemetery Ridge, just south of town. Buford kept the Confederates at bay long enough to fall back along the ridge lines—from Herr's Ridge to McPherson's Ridge, to Seminary Ridge, and finally to Cemetery Ridge. In doing so, Buford helped the Union secure the valuable high ground that he had scouted earlier.

If he had won a victory on any of the earlier ridges, he certainly would have taken it and pressed his advantage. However, he might not have been able to hold any of those positions if he hadn't defied the odds and attacked when dramatically outnumbered. By ultimately securing the high ground on Cemetery Ridge, Buford's bold actions gave the Union the tactical advantage to win the battle and, ultimately, turn the tide of the war.

A Calculated Technology Risk

A contemporary example of a leader who was willing to defy the odds was Steve Jobs, CEO of Apple. The evolution of Apple in the twenty-first century is the story of a struggling competitor in the personal computer market that became the arbiter of technology and culture around the globe. Jobs, the mercurial founder of Apple, positioned the company for success by following the same steps John Buford did and taking similar calculated risks.

From its roots as a single participant in the cutthroat personal computer market in the 1970s, by the turn of the millennium, Apple was not only an industry leader, but also the pioneer in a cultural revolution that used technology to alter life patterns and overhaul entire industries.

Jobs famously founded Apple computers in his garage with friend and partner Steve Wozniak in 1976. The partners worked to make Apple one of the fiercest competitors in the hardware industry, which included IBM, Microsoft, and Dell. During the 1980s, this group of companies established personal computers as a common luxury item. As CEO of Apple from 1976 to 1985, Jobs, with Wozniak, searched for a way to stay competitive in this increasingly crowded market. To that end, Jobs aggressively pushed himself, and his employees, to break the rules, do things differently, and defy the odds.

By 1985, Jobs's obsession with taking risks had gotten him fired from the company he founded. He started other companies, including NeXT, a platform that specialized in computers for higher education and business markets. Jobs also shifted his focus from hardware to software, and even became the driving force behind the formation of Pixar Animation Studios. During his time with NeXT and Pixar, Jobs's focus sharpened to consumer electronics, which he defined more broadly than the standard personal computer. Companies like IBM, Microsoft, Dell, and, yes, Apple (minus Jobs) spent much of the 1990s working on innovations to make PCs easier to use and navigate, while Jobs explored new roles for technology in all areas of life.

In 1997, Apple had lost its competitive edge and was on the brink of bankruptcy. The board of directors invited Jobs back as CEO. They realized they needed Jobs's innovative, out-of-the-box thinking. Jobs agreed that innovation had to happen, but he developed a new purpose for the company—to redefine how people interacted with technology. Jobs quoted Henry Ford's famous adage about the automobile: "If I had asked people what they wanted, they'd have said a faster horse."

Armed with this new purpose, Jobs set aggressive goals for innovation. He took stock of his resources—particularly his human and creative resources. Working at Apple became synonymous with being on the cutting edge of creativity and workplace culture. Because of his experience with Pixar, Jobs had a deep understanding of the power of technology to tell stories. He extrapolated this understanding to reenvision how technology can impact lives, and he created systems and resources to do exactly that.

Jobs surveyed the competition, many of whom were his good friends and collaborators. He realized that they were continuing to innovate in what he saw as an outdated paradigm. Rather than meet them on their own terms, Jobs created new products and markets that his competitors didn't even know existed. In some cases, Jobs created entire markets that no one in the industry even believed were necessary.

Jobs's mastery came with recognizing the importance of a tipping point. Everything he did was based on small changes that made a big difference. He completely reconceptualized the user interface. He observed small things people did intuitively with their devices—like shaking them when they made a typing error—and turned them into standard features. He recognized the importance of design and the feel of the device in the user's hand as a crucial element of sales. On the face of it, these are all small things, but they made a huge difference to the cumulative Apple experience.

Finally, Jobs was proactive. He didn't wait for a competitor to create a product and then rush to build a better one. He imagined how people could use technology—to listen to music, to take pictures—and incorporated these functions into, of all things, a mobile telephone. Before he launched a new product, he made sure he had supply lines in place for at least a decade to ensure that Apple never had shortages. He looked at ways that technology could be more integrated into daily life and instigated demand by creating devices around those activities, rather than waiting until a need arose. By thinking several steps ahead—like buying glass screens from China before the market moved there—he was able to secure resources long before going to market.

Rather than take the safe path and improve products already offered by competitors, Jobs defied the odds by inventing devices no one knew they needed. Sony had a robust market presence in portable music players, and Blackberry was the leader in personal digital assistants. Consumers were not demanding a better way and the market in these areas was by no means saturated. Jobs, however, calculated the odds of success by entering these traditional sectors and, instead, defied those odds by innovating not only new devices, but new cultural and organizational behavior patterns.

What can you learn from Steve Jobs and General John Buford? Because Buford defied the odds, he was able to ensure an advantageous position for the Union and help turn the tide of the Civil War. The result of Steve Jobs defying the odds was the iPod, iPhone, iPad, and iTunes, which revolutionized the telecommunications, music and film industries and changed lives around the world.

When faced with rapidly changing environments, these individuals set the example of being willing to assess everything, plan out options, and take the most audacious one. Defy the odds and you position your team for the greatest advantage, regardless of what changes come at you.

Exercises for Defying the Odds

- Reconnect with your organization's purpose. Write out a purpose statement or revise the one you have. Read it daily.
- Review your systems. Are they effective? Are you doing things the way they've always been done? Are your team members empowered to innovate?

- Inventory your resources. Where are you heavy? Where are you light? Can you reallocate anything to be more effective?
- Evaluate your competitors. Have they made moves in the past twelve months that merit your attention? If so, is there anything for you to do about it?
- Brainstorm five small actions you can do to make a big difference.
- Look at your organization, inside and out. Where do you see current trends going in six months? A year? Five years? What would you do in those cases?
- In what areas can you take a calculated risk that will better position your team for success?

4

Do the Unexpected

When you least expect it, expect it.
—ANONYMOUS

Audacious strategies call for thinking outside the box. In the last chapter, Steve Jobs and Brigadier General John Buford defied the odds to perfectly position their organizations for success. A similar strategy for navigating change is to do the unexpected. When faced with change, the first impulse is typically to revert to predictable ways of doing things. It is easy to slide into comfort zones when you feel threatened. Great leaders—audacious leaders—know when to do the unexpected.

Doing the unexpected doesn't mean panicking or flying by the seat of your pants. It means having the emotional intelligence and relationship-building skills to lead people in uncertain situations. In times of change, your team feels as if *everything* is unexpected. Your job as a leader is to put them at ease, and you do that by building trust. Team members who trust their leaders feel confident and secure, even in the face of rapidly changing, stressful conditions. When you take the time to build relationships based on trust, your team will follow you audaciously into the abyss of the unexpected.

Building trust takes time. It is easier to achieve trust when things are calm and routines are secure. Once change begins, people's equilibrium is upset. It is difficult to build a strong foundation on shifting ground, but it's not impossible. If your company is not in the midst of change, take advantage of it and work to deepen the trust within your team. If you're already in the thick of a transition, fear not. Building trust is still possible. Change goes more smoothly when trust is well established, but it's never too late to start.

I learned this firsthand. I took over as the leader of a small nonprofit that had severe trust issues. My predecessor had been brilliant as an individual contributor but had problems building an effective and functional team dynamic. Less than a month before I took over as the new executive, my predecessor and the board restructured staff roles. No one was happy with the changes.

It was incredibly difficult to build trust, both between myself and the staff and among staff members, against the backdrop of this major change. It took close to a year before we stopped wasting time and energy on the very basics of an organization—believing that colleagues were capable, feeling safe to ask for help, or sharing a new project. It took time, patience, and a lot of uncomfortable conversations, but we finally created a high-performing team.

Skills for Building Trust

Building trust during chaos takes outstanding emotional intelligence (EQ) skills. Whereas the first strategy, lean into it, highlighted the need for personal emotional intelligence skills, this strategy requires greater proficiency in the social EQ skills, which are social awareness and relationship management. These crucial skills include transparency, integrity, clarity, empathy, and inspiration.

Let's begin with **transparency**. Trust requires information, especially in a changing environment. A savvy leader shares as much information as possible with everyone involved. In a major change, giving your team as much accurate information as possible keeps rumors and gossip from taking over.

Additionally, it's not enough to communicate that everything is being done in a new way. It's critically important to reiterate the why. People feel secure when they understand there's a positive reason for the upheaval, and that the change will create an ultimate benefit. When they get a glimpse into the decision-making process, and are included where appropriate, it helps followers trust their leaders and eases the impact of transitions.

In big changes, such as a merger or a new strategic plan, it might be tempting to hold information close to the vest for fear of upsetting staff or playing into unfounded fears. However, this secrecy usually backfires. In the absence of real information, people make up all sorts of stories.

It is better to be completely transparent about all of it—the easy decisions *and* the tough ones—than to try to protect people. It's also perfectly reasonable to admit that you don't have an answer or that something is still in process. When you treat people like children by withholding information, they usually act like children—tantrums, arguments, and overall childishness. However, if you expect them to act like adults in the face of change, they rise to the occasion. When given transparent answers and included in decisions, even tough ones, team members trust leaders more and become steadfast allies.

The second factor to building trust is **integrity**. When you are a leader, everything you think, say, and do must match. If it doesn't, your team will know it. You might ask, "Why does what I think matter? No one knows what I'm thinking." That's not true. You have opinions that leak out all the time. They may show up as offhand comments, facial expressions, or jokes you tell. Regardless, people can tell what you think. You've probably known someone who said one thing and did another. This hypocritical behavior undermines trust, rather than builds it.

The word *integrity* is an engineering term that means "to be structurally sound." Although it is used as a synonym for *honesty*, it has a deeper dimension. Nothing can be structurally sound if the foundation is out of alignment with the building on top of it. The foundation of everything is your values.

When your thoughts match your values, your foundation is structurally sound. Your actions and words will match your thoughts, whether you are aware of it or not. Consequently, integrity shows when what you say and what you do line up with your thoughts and values. When you operate from integrity, you telegraph that you are trustworthy.

Once you are sure you're operating from integrity, the next quality you need to build trust is **clarity**, particularly in communication. Communication is more than giving directions and sending effective memos. As the idea of authenticity has crept into leadership philosophy, some managers believe that authentic communication excuses angry outbursts, clumsy directives, or inappropriate sharing. Communication is a more complicated endeavor, however.

According to studies done by psychologist Albert Mehrabian at UCLA in the 1960s, when listening to a voice reading a single word, only 7 percent of the meaning is determined by the actual content of what you're saying. Your tone of voice and facial expressions make up another 38 percent, and a whopping 55 percent of communication is body language. Similarly, body language expert Ray Birdwhistell estimated in the 1970s that between 60 percent and 75 percent of communication is nonverbal.

Although Mehrabian's and Birdwhistell's work have been hotly debated over the decades, it seems obvious that nonverbal communication is an important part of imparting meaning. This is why texting and email communications are less clear than in-person communications. For a short message to convey a quick answer or confirm a time or place, texting and email are fine. For any sort of nuanced communication, you must do it in person.

One of my favorite stories about the pitfalls of content-only communication comes from a friend of mine while she was dating her husband. They were having a long-distance relationship, and he had flown to see her for a long weekend. Toward the end of the weekend, she started to get a cold, and it continued to get worse until, by the time she put him on the plane home on Sunday night, she was feeling terrible.

After she dropped him off at the airport, she thought about their growing relationship and realized she didn't know what he was like when he was sick. Men are notoriously either complete babies or stoic to a fault, and she wondered which of these described the new man in her life. Knowing she couldn't talk to him because he was in-flight, she texted him an innocent question, asking, "What *kind* of a sick person are you? [emphasis added]." She went to bed.

He landed a few hours later, and because he knew she would be asleep, he didn't bother to call. When he arrived home, he took out his phone to text her a sweet message and saw her text, "What kind of a *sick person* are you? [emphasis added]." Of course, he immediately called to see what he'd done wrong that would lead her to be angry with him. It's laughable now, but this case of clumsy communication is a great example of how important tonality, expression, and body language are to clarity.

While clarity in communication is always a good policy, it is crucial during transitions. It is better to over-communicate than under-communicate. You must communicate with every party involved. Continually reiterate *why* changes are happening and what's being done about them. It is important that, even if it doesn't seem like there is anything substantive to talk about, you send updates and confirmations of what's already been decided. It is also critical to communicate in all directions, not just from the top down. Create channels for staff to talk to leaders and forums for colleagues and peers to share ideas and concerns.

The most important part of clarity in communication, however, is not necessarily what you say, but how well you listen. People rarely practice listening skills. Too often, communicating means telling, and listening means waiting to speak. If you have ever politely stared at another person, waiting for their lips to stop moving so that you can jump in with your brilliant response, you know what I mean. However, a study published in 2016 in the *Harvard Business Review* showed that employees felt more engaged with leaders who listened carefully than with those who spoke definitively. Seeking first to understand, *then* to be understood, is the hallmark of excellent communication.

Fourth, leaders build trust by having **empathy**. Team members trust leaders whom they believe understand them. This doesn't mean getting caught up in everyone else's drama, but it does entail putting yourself in your team members' shoes to think about how changes impact them. Listening to concerns without trying to give advice or take sides shows you care about each team member as a person. Imagining how the changes will impact team members gives you credibility and a platform to build a strong relationship.

Because change affects everyone differently, creating new structures, policies, or procedures while expecting everyone to adapt uniformly is naive at best and disastrous at worst. Empathy helps leaders know all team members are moving forward toward a common goal. During times of transition, conflict arises as team members see an opportunity to assert their own viewpoints or agendas. A leader who is empathetic manages the complex relationships and navigates potential conflicts, so each team member establishes common ground and moves forward productively.

Finally, trust comes from **inspiration**. Humans are drawn toward hope. Although a leader builds trust by being transparent, having integrity, and being empathetic and clear, at the moment of truth, great leaders inspire. They inspire with their words, by building confidence in the team and reiterating the belief they will always succeed. They inspire with action by moving toward a productive outcome. When a team feels the energy of the leader's passion and witnesses the depth of the leader's commitment, their own doubts dissolve and they are inspired to follow.

Practicing transparency, integrity, clarity, empathy, and inspiration builds a foundation of trust. During calm, steady times, the foundation of trust creates cohesive, respectful, innovative teams. During times of transition, however, this trust is the cornerstone of one of the most audacious strategies for navigating change—doing the unexpected. To do the unexpected takes incredibly tight teamwork, however, since everyone must pull in the same direction, *away* from what is safe, easy, and predictable. Doing the counterintuitive thing takes an act of will, but can be a winning strategy.

One way to do the unexpected is to expand when the market is contracting. For example, my husband and I own a small chain of fast-casual pizza restaurants. When the COVID-19 pandemic hit, many restaurants didn't survive the shutdown. During the crisis, we were offered the opportunity to expand into two new markets. We evaluated the opportunities, discussed them with our team—who trusted us because of years of practicing transparency, integrity, clarity, empathy, and inspiration—and expanded. Despite contracting market conditions, we navigated the challenge by doing the unexpected.

A common example of doing the unexpected is going on the offensive when common sense dictates a defensive position. You've probably heard the phrase, "the best defense is a strong offense," which is really another way of saying that doing the unexpected works.

Leading into the Unexpected with Trust

During the Battle of Gettysburg, one of the greatest historical examples of doing the unexpected was Colonel Joshua Lawrence Chamberlain and the 20th Maine regiment.

Chamberlain was a professor of rhetoric at Bowdoin College when the Civil War started. An ardent abolitionist, he defied the school administration and his family's wishes and volunteered for the army in 1862. His first engagement was at the Battle of Fredericksburg in December 1862, where he participated in some of the bloodiest fighting of that battle.

By the time of the Battle of Gettysburg in July 1863, Chamberlain was the commanding officer of the 20th Maine. He had been in the Army of the Potomac less than a year and had commanded the regiment only a few days. The regiment started with over 1,000 men but was down to one-third its strength, about 300 troops. On the morning of July 2 Chamberlain was camped in northern Maryland. He had been sick for several days. To make matters worse, that morning he was given the responsibility of guarding approximately 120 mutineers—Union soldiers from a different Maine regiment who were refusing to fight.

Given that Chamberlain's command had fewer than 300 men, he was tasked with guarding a contingent of troublemakers a third the size of his loyal troops. The guards told Chamberlain that the mutineers had signed three-year enrollment papers and now wanted out early. Chamberlain was to guard them until they could appear for a court-martial. At that exact moment, Chamberlain received orders that the Union Army was engaged with the Confederates, and his troops were moving out to join the fight.

In this rapidly changing environment, with new people in leadership, disengaged troops to guard, and a battle looming, Chamberlain had to make sure that the 20th Maine was the most cohesive fighting unit it could be. He understood that his ability to lead them effectively balanced on trust. To build that trust, Chamberlain had to utilize every step just discussed.

First, he was transparent. He believed it was ridiculous to force a man to fight at gunpoint, as with the mutineers, and told them so. He dismissed the guards and explained the mutineers' options. He asked the mutineers when they'd last eaten and, upon learning they hadn't been fed in days, immediately got them food. He agreed to meet with their spokesperson while making it clear they were moving out soon. He admitted outright that there was nothing he could do about their situation at that moment. He promised that, after the battle, he would do whatever he could to be sure they were treated fairly.

Second, he embodied integrity. He modeled his own values of respect and fairness. He fed them. He promised to hear their grievances. He met with their elected spokesperson to understand what was wrong. He honestly told them that he wasn't going to shoot them—a threat that other commanders had used frequently—and assured them that he would see that they got fair treatment. His beliefs and his words and his actions all matched.

Third, he had clarity. He realized how desperately his regiment could use 120 seasoned fighters. He knew he wanted the mutineers to join the 20th Maine and acted from that premise. He communicated with amazing clarity, paying particular attention to listening. He met with the spokesperson for the mutineers privately. He listened to his problem, which turned out not to be three-year enlistment papers. They were upset about the dissolution of their regiment, the 2nd Maine.

Multiple other commanders had the opportunity to turn the mutineers around, but none of them listened to find out what was really wrong. Chamberlain repeated back what he heard until he believed he understood the problem, which was treatment that showed a lack of respect and appreciation. He said virtually nothing during this first meeting. He just listened.

He then spoke to the mutineers as a group, where he exhibited great empathy. He began by letting them know that he understood why they were upset and that he agreed with their grievances. He reflected back what he had heard and told them he would do what he could to resolve their problems. He clearly explained his situation—not having enough troops—and asked for their help by acknowledging the sacrifices they had already made. He treated them with the respect he could see they wanted.

Finally, he inspired them. He communicated why they were fighting and reminded them that they were there because they believed in a common goal of a free union—not divided into free states and slave states. He reminded them that there was a greater vision at work in what they were doing. He offered them a win-win solution.

Since the 20th Maine was down to a third of its strength, he invited the mutineers to fight with his regiment. He told them if they fought, all the charges against them would be dropped. They would get their muskets back and no more would be said about it. He offered them the choice of coming along under guard or coming along as active parts of the regiment. He allowed them some time to decide, and all but three joined the 20th Maine.

Chamberlain's steps to build trust were a crucial foundation for what came next. Within hours, he would ask these men to do something so unexpected and so audacious that it altered the course of history. He couldn't have done it without the trust he took time to build.

As soon as the 20th Maine left camp, they marched ten miles and went right into battle, positioned on the extreme left of the Union line, on top of a rocky point called Little Round Top. They faced concerted attacks from the 15th and 47th Alabama, losing men at a rapid rate. They were ordered, however, to defend the position "at all hazards," meaning they could not retreat under any circumstances. After five attacks by the

Alabamians, the 20th Maine was out of ammunition and bunched nearly in a circle as the Confederates kept trying to get around their left flank.

Here, Chamberlain ordered the unexpected. At a point when any other commander might have surrendered or ordered a retreat, Chamberlain ordered an almost-suicidal bayonet charge down the hill, attacking the oncoming Alabamians. Most men don't like fighting with bayonets—it's too close and takes a lot of specialized training—but because Chamberlain built trust among the disparate parts of his regiment, he was able to succeed with the charge.

The 20th Maine, including the mutineers, saved Little Round Top and is credited with saving the entire Union left flank. For this act, Chamberlain was one of the first recipients of the Congressional Medal of Honor.

Building an Empire on Trust

Doing the unexpected doesn't have to be as dramatic as Chamberlain at Gettysburg. Sometimes, it just means following a gut instinct that flies in the face of conventional wisdom. Power couple Chip and Joanna Gaines, founders of the Magnolia empire, provide an example from the business world. They did the unexpected by leaving their hit TV show, which was the platform of their success, just as they were launching multiple complementary businesses.

I was a huge fan of their HGTV show *Fixer Upper*, which ran for five seasons from 2013 to 2018. Like most of their fans, I was shocked when I heard that right after opening their retail mecca in Waco, Texas, they left the show. I sadly read predictions that their empire would crumble.

However, Chip and Joanna were doing the unexpected. In Chip Gaines's book, *No Pain, No Gaines*, he outlined what led them to do the unexpected. Through their careers in the real estate and home improvement business, they built a large network of people who contributed to their success, and they did it by building trust. They regularly practiced transparency with their team, bringing team members together for planning and strategy sessions. They strove to do everything with integrity, making sure the businesses ran according to their values.

When I visited The Silos in Waco, I was surprised that they were closed on Sunday, an important day in retail. Their values, however, dictate a day of rest, so they close. They have clarity of purpose and practice it in their communications, which now includes a quarterly publication, *The Magnolia Journal*. They empathize with their staff, their clients, and their audience, and portray it in their TV series.

Finally, they inspire everyone around them—staff, clients, and audiences (read the Magnolia Manifesto as one of the greatest examples of a mission statement *ever*). They did the unexpected and succeeded, with growing their retail area, writing books, and launching their own network.

Doing the unexpected is purposely placed in the middle of these steps, because it relies on trust, which is the fulcrum on which all the ways leading through change are balanced. Without building trust, a leader is either out of balance toward their own agenda or too heavily leaning toward others. It is only by building trust that change becomes an evolutionary experience, rather than a disaster.

Doing the unexpected is a sure-fire strategy for navigating transitions. Whether it's expanding during a pandemic, going on the offense when outnumbered, or walking away at the height of success, the unexpected gives leaders the freedom to see change as a catalyst rather than a catastrophe.

Exercises for Doing the Unexpected

- Outline the predictable path to success in your industry. In what ways have you followed it? How have you diverged from it?

- List three ways you can practice greater transparency with your team.
- What are your values? List three examples where you act with integrity with those values. In what areas can you be in greater integrity?
- Do you know what inspires your people? Research inspirational stories that can apply to your industry and keep them in a file.
- Practice listening. Make it a point to focus on the other person's every word. Repeat back to them what you heard them say.
- Write a short, clear directive for your team. Continue to edit until you are completely clear. The shorter, the better.
- List three areas where you might be called to do the unexpected. Marketing? Sales? Staffing?

5

Know When to Do Nothing

Grant me the serenity to accept the things I cannot change, courage to change the things I can, and the wisdom to know the difference.

—Reinhold Niebuhr

As powerful, effective, and audacious as it can be to do the unexpected, it is sometimes even more audacious to simply do nothing. Doing nothing requires you, as a leader, to take a counterintuitive step. Change causes a period of chaos, and the way most people respond to chaos is to act.

You have probably heard the overused phrase "don't just sit there, do something!" It seems obvious that if you want something to be better, you must make it happen. This works in so many contexts that it has become the default frame of mind. Therefore, when you are faced with a stressful transition or placed in a rapidly changing environment, your natural reaction is to take action to control the circumstances. There is nothing wrong with this strategy—when it works. Sometimes, however, circumstances are so far beyond your control that "doing something" is just spinning your wheels and wasting time and resources that you can conserve by watching and waiting.

The ancient teaching of Taoism called the strategy of doing nothing wu wei, which means "non-doingness" or not to act. Taoists believe that perfect action is sometimes inaction. In Chinese tradition, emperors were supposed to lead through wu wei, which mandated that they evaluate all possible outcomes before acting.

The Five Elements for Doing Nothing

In studying wu wei, I identified five basic leadership elements necessary to manage change by doing nothing: trust your team, identify your strengths, avoid the cycle of escalating commitment, be willing to sustain losses, and practice personal restraint.

The first piece of doing nothing is **trusting your team.** I refer to the trust-building measures discussed in the previous chapter: a leader's best strategy through change is to be transparent and collaborative with team members. Tell them frankly that things are going to change. When people know what to expect, they are more likely to embrace change.

This strategy, however, takes trust a step further and requires you, as the leader, to trust your team. Learn each member's strengths, weaknesses, abilities, and proclivities so you can predict how each will act under pressure. If you have built this team yourself, you probably already trust them. If you inherited this team, you may need to invest some time to build trust. People will rise to the level of your expectations.

Next, **identify your strengths.** Take stock of your resources, your position, and your assets. To do nothing, leaders must be sure that they are in a strong enough position to weather the storm. Fear of the future can easily cloud your vision so that you only see what's missing. When that happens, negative outcomes seem to be everywhere. By creating an inventory of strengths, you counteract the negativity and build confidence in your ability to stay the course.

Knowing when to do nothing also means ascertaining how to **avoid the cycle of escalating commitment.**

This cycle is a pattern of human behavior where an individual or group refuses to change tactics, despite increasingly negative outcomes. Anecdotally, this is referred to as "throwing good money after bad" or "in for a penny, in for a pound." However, one of my personal favorite phrases for avoiding the cycle of escalating commitment is this one: "when you're at the bottom of a hole, stop digging."

The cycle starts because you allowed your ego to keep you from admitting an error. If you must be right at all costs, watch for the cycle of escalating commitment. Your best bet is to periodically step away and ask what would happen if you simply gave up.

The fourth element of doing nothing is to determine your team's level of risk tolerance. Changes mean **incurring losses**, even if the change is positive. Many leaders, myself included, have implemented staff reorganizations or strategic initiatives that were exciting and progressive, but also required layoffs or department closures.

Leaders must be prepared for the consequences of the losses. As hard as it is to sustain losses, savvy leaders realize that they usually open the way for greater opportunity. Change also brings added benefits, and it's up to you to decide whether they were worth the losses. In business, the most common losses are clients, programs, and employees.

I had to learn this lesson the hard way. In my first marketing business, I was desperate to get clients. I was a single parent and started my business without enough capital to get me through the first year. When I got a client, I offered whatever service they wanted, just to get paid. I justified this because it felt like I was being conscientious and offering outstanding customer service.

As I got more clients, I was able to relax and stick with the services listed on my rate sheet. However, my first two clients continued to demand more than I could reasonably offer for what they were paying me. At first, I was terrified to incur a loss, so I kept doing the work.

After about three months, I found that these two clients were taking more time than all my higher-paying clients combined, and the extra "free" work was keeping me from servicing other clients or soliciting new business. I had gotten myself into the cycle of escalating commitment and I had to correct it. If I either raised my rates or reduced my services, I might lose them, but I had to be willing to incur the loss or nothing would change.

Being willing to incur losses doesn't mean you *will* incur them. Frequently, the things you fear most never happen. I talked to my clients about my dilemma. One of them was upset and ended our contract, but the other one completely understood and stuck with me for years. The client who ended the contract referred someone to me who ended up being a great client.

By being willing to suffer the loss, you can make decisions that are in the best interest of the organization without feeling compromised or constricted by making decisions to please or protect individuals.

Finally, to know when to do nothing, you must practice **heroic self-control.** When change is raging all around, your jittery team will want to do something. At best, their tendency will be to swing into productive action. At worst, they will blindly panic. Either way, your level of self-control as a leader sets the tone for the effectiveness of this strategy. When using the strategy of doing nothing, a leader must practice self-control and cool confidence. You must be able to watch events play out and react moderately and appropriately.

A time will come for action. The strategy of knowing when to do nothing has a limited shelf life. At some point, action will be required. The trick is to know when to wait and when to act. Furthermore, when it is time to act, take only *inspired* action. Inspired action will have immediate, short-term impact and significant long-term benefits, compared to action for the sake of staying busy. This is the difference between throwing spaghetti at the wall to see what sticks and thoroughly weighing options, waiting for the right time to move.

Knowing When to Do Nothing at Gettysburg

To illustrate this point from a historical perspective, let's return to the Battle of Gettysburg and look at one of the most poignant episodes of the entire battle, Pickett's Charge.

The story of Pickett's Charge is almost always told from the viewpoint of the Confederacy, with good reason. When seen from the South's perspective, it is a cautionary tale of the dangers of pride and arrogance.

General Robert E. Lee came to Gettysburg following a series of stunning successes in which he prevailed against overwhelming odds. Because of these stellar victories, Lee was overconfident in his abilities and disparaging about his opponents. However, Lee had lost the great corps commander, Stonewall Jackson, at the Battle of Chancellorsville just two months earlier, leaving Lee with untested commanders in crucial positions.

Additionally, Lee's cavalry left him without crucial information until two-thirds of the way through the battle, forcing him to guess at the other side's strength and position. Despite these factors, Lee disregarded the opinion of his second-in-command, General James Longstreet, and ordered the infamous Pickett's Charge.

By the third day of the battle, General Lee had attacked the Union Army from the left and the right, and although the Confederates had won victories, they had not yet been able to give the decisive knockout punch. Lee believed that the Union Army was concentrated on each end of its line—a response to the pattern of fighting the previous day. That meant their weakest point should be in the center. He came up with a plan to use a fresh division under General George Pickett to attack the center of the line and hopefully defeat the Union.

Longstreet advised against the plan. As Lee's second-in-command, Longstreet saw the risks involved and was unenthusiastic, to say the least. Tactically, he believed that Lee was asking the men to do the impossible. The troops would have to march almost a mile over open ground, with no cover of trees or buildings. They would be marching uphill straight into artillery fire, and for the last 100 yards they had to charge facing troops hidden behind a stone wall, taking intense rifle fire.

Assuming any of the Confederate troops made it over the wall, there would be no reinforcements to take advantage of the inroad. Lee, however, ordered the attack, which has become synonymous with heroic failure.

Although studying Pickett's Charge from the Confederates' point of view is a cautionary tale, it is equally instructive to view the episode from the Union position. For the first two days of the battle, momentum had been on the side of the Confederacy, but the Union line had stubbornly refused to break.

Thanks to the excellent position scouted on July 1 by General John Buford and occupied by General Winfield Scott Hancock, and the heroic bayonet charge on Little Round Top by Colonel Joshua Lawrence Chamberlain with the 20th Maine on July 2, the Union thwarted any meaningful Confederate gains in two days of fighting.

On the night of July 2–3, Union General George G. Meade held a council of war with all his generals. They had been attacked on both flanks. Most of the generals anticipated that Lee's next move would be to attack them in the middle of the line. In this council, Meade implemented the audacious strategy of knowing it was time to do nothing.

First, he trusted his team, particularly General Winfield Hancock, whose corps would take the brunt of the attack. As the commanders weighed in, they were reluctant to leave their fortified position to initiate an attack but felt confident in their ability to repulse one. Meade trusted their assessment. Although Meade had only been in command of the Army of the Potomac for a few days, he had been a corps commander and friend of his subordinates for years. It was easy for him to trust them because of their long-standing relationship.

Second, Meade identified his strengths. He took inventory of his troops, artillery, cavalry, ammunition, and, most of all, his position on the high ground. Meade was an engineer by training, which served him well in assessing his resources. He agreed that they had an incredibly strong position and more troops in reserve. He also counted that intangible resource—his army's desire to defeat Lee and the soldiers who had humiliated them so many times over the past year.

Third, Meade recognized that Lee was caught in the cycle of escalating commitment. Meade knew his opponent well and correctly anticipated that he wouldn't be able to back down. Rather than wasting his soldiers' energy fighting in the open, Meade allowed his opponent to do it. His men would conserve their energy and ammunition and allow the Confederates to wear themselves out climbing the hill and attacking the stone wall.

Fourth, Meade was willing to sustain losses. No commander relishes sending troops to their death, but Meade was a seasoned officer, and he knew the stakes were high for him to win this battle. The Union Army could have pulled out under the cover of darkness and retreated to a position that would have, perhaps, baited the South to follow, but there was no guarantee. This tactic might have saved lives in the short term, but it would have delayed the inevitable confrontation and possibly prolonged the war, causing greater casualties in the long run. Because he was willing to take the risk of sustaining losses, Meade stood his ground.

Finally, Meade and all the Union commanders exhibited spectacular personal control. Pickett's Charge was preceded by a two-hour-long cannonade that rattled everyone's nerves. General Meade was eating lunch at his headquarters about a half mile behind the front line when a cannon ball came through the roof and killed an aide. Meade quietly stood up and calmly mounted his horse to move farther back.

Similarly, commanders on the front lines modeled calm for their soldiers. General Alexander Webb was a perfect example of composure. Webb's brigade was in the center of the Union line against Pickett's Charge. As the Confederates launched their massive artillery barrage, Webb made himself conspicuous to his men. He stood in front of the line and leaned on his sword, puffing leisurely on a cigar while cannonballs whistled by and shells exploded all around.

General Alexander Hays, positioned nearby, had his men calmly gather and load rifles discarded by the wounded and stack them neatly so they would have them handy when needed. The epitome of self-control was General Winfield Hancock, who rode prominently along the battle lines as the Confederates approached, and even after being wounded in the groin, he refused to be moved to a medical station until the battle was decided.

Each of these men waited patiently, seemingly doing nothing, as the Confederates approached. At the appropriate time, they opened fire and thus carried the day.

The Union strategy of knowing when to do nothing paid off. They ultimately took action, but their patience in waiting for the attack was key to their success. Although the Union suffered about 1,500 casualties during Pickett's Charge, that was only about 20 percent of their total force. The figure was negligible compared to their opponents' losses. The Confederates had over 6,000 casualties, approximately 50 percent, and lost an entire midlevel of leadership.

Although Lee and the Confederates fought for two more years, they never recovered from Pickett's

Charge. Meade knew when to do nothing and, consequently, let the Confederacy knock itself out.

Doing Nothing in Dallas

A more contemporary illustration of knowing when to do nothing is an episode called the Malice in Dallas. In 1990, quirky Southwest Airlines CEO Herb Kelleher approved a new tag line for the company, "Just Plane Smart." Unbeknownst to Kelleher and his team, a South Carolina–based aircraft sales company named Stevens Aviation had already trademarked the line.

Lawyers for Stevens Aviation urged their CEO, Kurt Herwald, to sue Southwest over the infringement. Although Southwest didn't have exceedingly deep pockets at that time, it was likely that Stevens would get a generous settlement. However, the court battle would cost hundreds of thousands of dollars for an uncertain outcome.

Instead, Herwald decided to do nothing. He trusted his board of directors and marketing team to come up with a winning strategy. He identified Stevens Aviation's strengths, recognizing that they didn't compete in the same market as Southwest Airlines. He successfully avoided the cycle of escalating commitment, realizing Stevens Aviation could waste time, money, and energy on an uncertain court battle, or they could target their resources into something productive. He was willing to lose—in this case, I'll call it "share"—the use of his tag line.

Finally, rather than fly off the handle like the stereotype of a CEO, he exhibited commendable self-control. He calmly called Herb Kelleher and proposed a better solution.

Herwald suggested to Kelleher that the two men arm-wrestle for use of the tag line. Herwald realized that his smaller company might not have the financial wherewithal to win a court case against Southwest Airlines, so he created a win-win situation where he and Kelleher staged a charity publicity stunt.

On March 20, 1992, 4,500 employees and guests of the two companies gathered at the Dallas Sportatorium for the so-called Malice in Dallas, a play on the 1974 Muhammed Ali/George Foreman fight in Zaire called the Rumble in the Jungle. Nearly every news crew in Texas covered the arm-wrestling challenge.

The terms of the challenge were that the two CEOs would go the best of three rounds. The loser of each round donated $5,000 to the charity of the opponent's choice. The winner would get sole ownership of the "Just Plane Smart" slogan.

After many shenanigans and much showmanship, the younger and more fit Herwald won two of the three rounds. The Muscular Dystrophy Association received a donation of $10,000, and the Ronald McDonald House of Cleveland got $5,000. The CEOs agreed to share the slogan, and Stevens Aviation went from being a minor player in the industry to national prominence.

Herwald credits the company's subsequent success to the Malice in Dallas. "[My employees] were so proud of the company and so excited for the visibility that Malice in Dallas gave to their work," he told a reporter. "For months and years after the event, the change to company culture was palpable. Employees felt more connected to one another and to their work."

Like the Union during Pickett's Charge, Herwald used the successful strategy of knowing when to do nothing. If you trust your team, identify your strengths, avoid the cycle of escalating commitment, are willing to incur losses, and practice self-control, you can show that, sometimes, doing nothing does it all.

Exercises for Knowing When to Do Nothing

- Evaluate your relationship with team members. Whom do you trust most? Do you need to work on building trust with others?
- Review your resources. If a major change—like a pandemic—happened tomorrow, how long

could you weather the storm? Do you need to reallocate resources?

- Look for places where you might be in danger of getting caught in the cycle of escalating commitment. Are there projects or initiatives you may want to reconsider?

- Identify your risk tolerance. Where can you afford to incur losses? Where do you need to build in redundancies?

- Evaluate your emotional intelligence skill of self-management. Can you exhibit grace under fire? Can you maintain composure under pressure?

- What are the areas of your organization where you identify your greatest threats? Do you anticipate acting on those threats?

6

Act as If

Believe and act as if it were impossible to fail.
—CHARLES KETTERING

The final of the five audacious strategies builds on the emotional intelligence skills and discipline you learned in the previous chapters. This audacious strategy starts with the premise that your thoughts and beliefs create your reality by influencing your behavior.

In the twenty-first century, it is a well-proven fact that thoughts influence reality. It has been over a century since the first scientific experiments examined the role of intentions on outcomes. The seminal experiment, known as the double-slit experiment, showed that light is both a wave and a particle. When left on its own, light functions like a wave. When an observer comes along to measure it, the act of observation fixes it into a particle.

When Possibility Turns into Reality

This revelation led to the wonderfully named thought exercise of Schrödinger's cat, which fans of the TV show *Big Bang Theory* will recognize. When no one's looking, photons are a wave of possibility. When someone looks, they become particles of reality. The implications show that everything "real" and tangible has been fixed into position by observations and expectations. Thus, your perspective creates your experience.

People seem to know this anecdotally. Those with a positive attitude seem to have positive things happen, and those who are negative have a more difficult time. You have probably noticed that when you feel optimistic, things go better, and when you don't, they don't. Plenty of scientific, psychological, physiological, and philosophical experiments have proven this. Thoughts create reality—not just for individuals, but for the world, as well.

There's a wonderful joke that highlights this point. Three umpires go to a bar to have a beer after a game. The first umpire says, "There are balls, and there are strikes, and I call them as I see them." The second umpire says, "Well, there are balls and there are strikes, and I call them as *they are*." The third umpire looks at his colleagues, shakes his head a bit, and with a small smirk says, "Gentlemen, there are balls and there are strikes, but they ain't nothin' until I call 'em!"

Your attitudes and mindset dictate how you interpret events, and that interpretation, in turn, impacts your actions. Actions, of course, influence outcomes. Stressful situations resulting from rapid changes have tremendous impact on how individuals and teams respond. Because individual attitudes dictate interpretation, responses to change can vary widely within organizations, even within teams. It is up to leaders to provide an interpretation of events that influences attitudes and actions toward a positive outcome. I call this "acting as if."

As a leader, you get to model the attitude and behavior you expect from your team. You do that by *acting as if* the outcome you want has already happened.

Once an event has happened, its meaning isn't necessarily fixed in stone. Humans constantly reinterpret events and reassign meaning based on current situations. Have you ever faced an adversity that, in the moment, felt like the end of the world? If so, you know that five years later, your idea of that event was much different than it was at the time. Events don't carry a single fixed meaning unless you refuse to reinterpret them.

How to Act as If

There are several ways to implement the strategy of acting as if. The first is to operate from the equation E+R=O: Event + Response = Outcome. The event is whatever change is happening, whether you instigated it or not. It can be something exciting, like a new strategic plan, an organizational restructure, or a new product line, or something dreaded, such as a recession, a hostile takeover, or a global pandemic. Regardless, the change is the event. The faster you accept the event, the quicker you can move to the part that makes all the difference, which is your response.

There are many ways to respond to the event, all of which are within your control. One response is to blame the event. This is a common reaction, but usually not very useful. Another response is to try to undo the event. Another might be to ignore the event or, still another, to embrace the event.

You can choose your response based on the outcome you want. Since your response directly impacts the outcome in the equation, you get to gauge your reactions. You act as if when you practice having responses that are consistent with the desired outcome. Modulating your response to produce an outcome will probably take you out of your comfort zone, but it is worth it. When you take the time to evaluate your response, rather than react with a conditioned, knee-jerk impulse, you grow as a leader and a person. All learning is based on the ability to evaluate your responses and extrapolate outcomes.

In 1998, I was diagnosed with stage IV lymphoma. I was thirty-three years old and otherwise healthy. I was a vegetarian and an avid runner. I also had a three-year-old daughter. After the initial shock of the diagnosis, I committed to doing everything possible to survive. I spoke with a friend who had the same type of cancer I did, only a few years before. She told me, "Cancer may have shaved a few years off my life, but I made it through it." She clearly interpreted the event as a struggle that she survived, and her anticipated outcome was a shortened life-span.

At the time, I didn't think too much about it, but as I continued to go through treatment, I chose a different response. I interpreted cancer as a gift. As I discovered more of my unhealthy emotional patterns, I realized that it didn't matter how physically fit I was. My fear and worry were killing me, and I had to change. I decided cancer wouldn't shave years off my life—it would add some!

I had been a miserable, emotional wreck when I was diagnosed with cancer. There was no way I could continue to live with that level of stress. I chose to act as if this cancer was a wake-up call—a launch pad to a better life. In the twenty-plus years since then, I found that cancer was my greatest teacher. My response created the desired outcome, and my life is so much better.

Another way to act as if is to intentionally define meaning. Humans are meaning-making machines. People assign meaning to events and circumstances every day, usually without knowing they are doing it. When you assign meaning intentionally, however, you are most powerful.

Most people who view change as a new opportunity to make a positive difference are acting as if life is getting better, not worse. By consciously defining the meaning of events, that definition creates your future reality.

If your organization is having financial problems, for example, you have the choice of treating it as a setback, challenge, or problem to be overcome. Certainly, no one would fault you for seeing the dilemma that way. It's the most common view of this type of business situation. The key question is what long-term benefit does the situation serve? Will that interpretation make your team more effective, or will it make them more cautious? Will you be able to recruit top-notch talent, or will you have to settle for those who can't find work at "successful" companies? Will morale be better, or worse, with that definition of events?

On the other hand, if you interpret financial problems as a way to streamline operations, cut unnecessary costs, effectively meet market challenges, and innovate more skillfully, the financial challenge becomes a catalyst for success. Your team will feel far more effective, having succeeded in challenging times. They will gain confidence in their abilities, recognizing that they can thrive even in difficult circumstances. You can recruit top talent who want to be part of a team that wins, regardless of the circumstances. You will have acted as if this were a glorious opportunity rather than an adversity.

Finally, the strategy of acting as if means consciously telling a better story. All history is a story, and people tell stories in many ways. You get to tell the story the way you want events to be remembered. In the absence of information, people interpret events based on their own judgments, opinions, and fears. If you have defined meaning, you now need to communicate that meaning to all members of your team. Talk it up in staff meetings, tell your direct reports how excited you are, look for opportunities to point out how today's new challenge is helping get the outcome you're seeking, and make sure that you always end on a positive note.

Do not allow yourself the luxury of kvetching and complaining with your team. If you have an emotional charge about something, deal with it in private, talk to your family and friends, or hire a therapist. To act as if, you must become cheerleader-in-chief. Your team is looking to you for the certainty and confidence to get through the daily trials and stay positive about what's on the other side.

When you tell a better story, you are facilitating the evolutionary process. Remember the dialectic from the opening chapter? It explains how growth happens by challenging the status quo (thesis) with a change or opposition (antithesis) to create a new, elevated condition (synthesis). You accomplish the elevated situation by consciously watching for the dynamic and then telling a positive story when you begin to see it emerge.

Once you see the interplay between the thesis, the antithesis, and the new synthesis, acting as if depends on how you, as a leader, interpret events. Show your team the possibilities that can play out. Use savvy communications to disseminate information as widely as possible.

"Four score and seven years ago"

One of the greatest examples of acting as if was Abraham Lincoln and his famous Gettysburg Address. During the Civil War, he stayed focused on his objectives of union and freedom and never allowed himself to show his discouragement in public. Regardless of events, he carefully chose responses that produced the outcomes he wanted. As a corollary, he also learned when his responses failed to produce his desired outcomes and changed his strategy.

For example, Lincoln notoriously struggled with generals for the Union Army. After getting off to a rocky start with General George McClellan, Lincoln fired him following the Peninsula Campaign in 1862 and replaced him with General John Pope. However, Pope led the Army of the Potomac to an embarrassing defeat at the Battle of Second Bull Run, which caused Lincoln to waffle and rehire McClellan. McClellan, however, proceeded to blow a chance to destroy Lee's army at the Battle of Antietam, the bloodiest single day of the Civil War. Lincoln removed him again—this time for good. Lincoln learned that the only appropriate response to the event of military defeat was to hire aggressive generals to get the outcome he wanted.

Lincoln also acted as if by repeatedly and intentionally defining meaning. For example, in Lincoln's first inaugural address, he tackled the topic of secession, which had been discussed almost since the inception of the nation. Powerful Southern congressmen presented the idea of secession as a reasonable and logical way for states to resolve disputes over federal policy—to simply leave. In the first inaugural, Lincoln, with a litigator's skill, redefined the meaning of secession and clearly showed that it was a permanent step toward anarchy.

Finally, Lincoln was a notoriously gifted storyteller and frequently spun yarns to entertain, but also to educate. When Lincoln came to a setback, he used a folksy tale to provide meaning. For example, Lincoln met opposition for appointing Ulysses S. Grant as Lieutenant General. Critics claimed that Grant was known to drink too much, and it impaired his ability to lead. As always, Lincoln had a witty and pithy comeback. He told critics, "I like him. He fights. Let me know what brand he drinks so I can send a case to all my generals."

Lincoln's first and second inaugural addresses are some of the most hopeful, optimistic, and inspiring speeches ever given, which is amazing, considering he delivered them during the greatest crisis this nation ever endured.

One of the greatest examples of Lincoln's ability to act as if was his Gettysburg Address. There is a reason that, much to the chagrin of millions of school children, this short address is still considered a must-study in public schools. In it, Lincoln practiced E+R=O: he defined meaning and told a new story about the future of the United States. In his short, 272-word address, he set a vision for the Union that was not considered until Lincoln articulated it in November 1863 at Gettysburg.

Although today the Battle of Gettysburg is considered the turning point of the Civil War, it was not deemed such a brilliant success in the immediate aftermath. Since the Confederate Army survived and retreated to Virginia, many people, North and South, asked the profound question, "Was this massive battle in vain?" Other than defending Pennsylvania, the initial opinions of the battle concluded it achieved no long-term strategic purpose.

General George Meade, who commanded his troops brilliantly at Gettysburg, nevertheless allowed General Lee and the Confederates to slip back to Southern soil. Instead of destroying the army and ending the war, Meade followed cautiously and allowed the enemy to escape.

There were also 51,000 casualties. The town of Gettysburg, with a population of approximately 2,500 at the time, was completely devastated burying the dead and caring for the wounded. Hasty burials on the battlefield were soon exposed by rain or foraging animals, and the stench of death hung over the town for months. Every available building was used as a hospital. The first visitors arrived in Gettysburg shortly after the battle, looking for lost husbands, brothers, and sons and putting a burden on the already-strapped townspeople to offer hospitality.

Because of the number of dead, the governor of Pennsylvania, Andrew Curtain, requested that the federal government establish a national cemetery at Gettysburg, the first in the nation. He appointed a local lawyer, David Wills, to head a committee to design and unveil the new cemetery. Wills planned a great opening ceremony for November 19, 1863, about four and a half months after the battle. The dedication date was chosen to accommodate the schedule of the keynote speaker, Edward Everett. Everett was a former senator, governor of Massachusetts, US Secretary of State, and president of Harvard. President Lincoln was also invited to make "a few appropriate remarks."

In an era when the president rarely left Washington, DC, and particularly in a wartime crisis, Lincoln accepted the invitation. Lincoln traveled from Washington to Gettysburg via train on the evening of November 18, 1863, stayed with David Wills and his family, and then rode down Baltimore Street the next morning to the dedication.

Edward Everett, true to the oration style of his era, spoke for over two hours. His speech recalled events from the battle in detail and drew upon classical military themes to make his points. He spoke of the heroism of the Union commanders and the sacrifice of the troops. He did not try to interpret the meaning of the battle. He was very well received. When he finished, to thunderous applause, he was seated, and the next speaker approached the platform.

The crowd certainly expected Lincoln to speak for longer than he did. As a matter of fact, the only picture taken of Lincoln at Gettysburg was of the top of his head as he left the platform. Because cameras took so long to set up in the nineteenth century, the photographer did not even get a picture of him while he spoke his 272 words. Lincoln was on the stage for approximately two minutes.

Yet in that time, Lincoln acted as if the Battle of Gettysburg was the turning point of the war. Rather than classifying the battle as a bloody disaster, he said it was "a new birth of freedom." He called upon his listeners to be dedicated "to the cause which they who fought here have thus far so nobly advanced." He promised that "these dead shall not have died in vain."

Edward Everett later wrote to the president and told him, "I should be glad, if I could flatter myself that I came as near to the central idea of the occasion in two hours, as you did in two minutes."

It is a myth that Lincoln jotted his famous address on the back of an envelope while on the train. He thought carefully about what he wanted to say and the purpose his remarks would fulfill. He reviewed the events of the battle and articulated his response to create his desired outcome, which was renewed support for the war. He eschewed the long and dramatic style that Everett used so his response was clear and direct.

He also crafted the speech to define the meaning of the battle as a crucial benchmark, not a vain bloodbath. He used the opportunity to issue a midcourse correction of the war's objectives. On a few previous occasions, Lincoln had spoken on the theme that became the hallmark of the Gettysburg Address, which was making freedom a key objective of the war, rather than just holding the Union together. He saw the speech at Gettysburg as his opportunity to define the meaning of the battle as a "new birth of freedom." He did so subtly and brilliantly.

When the Civil War started in 1861, it was a war to simply preserve the Union. The main argument between North and South was whether the Constitution allowed the federal government to make laws that restricted rights within the states, notably the "property" right to slavery. The South believed they were fighting a noble cause, keeping a "foreign" power from taking their property rights. The North, however, was just fighting to maintain the status quo—a goal that, while worthy, did not inspire great passion.

The crux of the issue, although Southerners refused to admit it, was slavery. For over a century, the Civil War has been taught as a contest over states' rights, and I always ask the follow-up question, a state's right to do what? The answer, of course, is to own slaves.

When Lincoln signed the Emancipation Proclamation in 1862, he knew that it was a controversial first step toward defining the war in terms of freedom, rather than maintaining the Union. However, the Emancipation Proclamation was a wartime measure, packaged to diminish the South's ability to make war. It wasn't an overall mandate on the value of freedom, and it certainly didn't claim freedom as a war goal.

That changed in the Gettysburg Address. When Lincoln uttered the immortal words, "Four score and seven years ago," he was telling the story that would resonate with every listener. He hearkened back to 1776 and the signing of the Declaration of Independence, not 1787, with the creation of the Constitution. By referencing the Declaration, which "set forth on this continent a new nation, conceived in liberty and dedicated to the proposition that all men are created equal," Lincoln undermined the argument that the Civil War was about the Constitution and states' rights and said instead that it was about fighting for "a new birth of freedom."

Lincoln's speech electrified the North. Now, instead of fighting merely to keep states in the Union, Northern troops fought for freedom and to defend the ideals of the Founding Fathers. It created a reality that engaged the North and gave it vision and purpose. Instead of wondering if the Battle of Gettysburg and, by extension, the entire war, was a vain shedding of blood, the Northern public now backed it as a valiant effort to extend the freedoms to life, liberty, and the pursuit of happiness promised in the Declaration of Independence and end the institution of slavery that had been a bone of contention since the founding of the republic.

In his 272 words, Lincoln created the reality he wanted. Rather than having a public that was questioning, struggling, and adrift for lack of vision, he galvanized them by giving them the meaning they were seeking and crafting a new vision of the republic that would completely change the policy and culture of the United States for the century-and-a-half following the Civil War.

Redefining a New Story

One hundred and twenty years after the Gettysburg Address, Oprah Winfrey provided another great example of acting as if. After a meteoric rise to prominence as a news anchor and morning show host in Nashville and Baltimore, Oprah moved to Chicago in 1983 to host WLS-TV's morning show, *AM Chicago.* Within months after Winfrey's arrival, the show went from last place in the ratings to overtaking *Donahue* as the highest-rated talk show in Chicago. Movie critic Roger Ebert persuaded Oprah to sign a syndication deal with King World; the show was renamed *The Oprah Winfrey Show* and expanded to a full hour. The first episode was broadcast nationwide on September 8, 1986.

Oprah's show originally qualified as a tabloid talk show, a popular format in the 1980s. Tabloid shows gained ratings by featuring sensational topics, controversial guests, and more than a little conflict. One of Oprah's best-known competitors in the 1990s was Jerry Springer, whose show launched in 1991.

In the early 1990s, competition from Springer's show pushed Oprah to cover more sensational and controversial content, but Oprah always had a limit. She was more comfortable sharing stories of personal growth and social justice than the prurient shock-schlock of Springer's genre. The public seemed to have voted with their viewership in 1998, when Springer rocked the daytime talk-show world by beating Oprah in the ratings with his lurid story lines and on-air fistfights.

At this point, Oprah could have allowed this setback to force her to change her format to be more sensational, or she could have given up altogether. Instead, she chose to act as if she was still on top by presenting content she valued. If the event was to lose in the ratings to trash-TV, Oprah's response was to realign with her higher purpose and get in touch with her authentic style. Never at ease with the negativity of the talk-show genre, she chose a response that directly contradicted expectations. She halted all the controversial topics and focused solely on helping people live their best lives. This, of course, produced an outcome that allowed her to regain her ratings supremacy and ultimately become the Queen of All Media.

It took more than just choosing the appropriate response to an event. Oprah chose to define the meaning of her temporary ratings defeat as an opportunity to get clarity on her true purpose. It might have been easy for her to get discouraged at the dismal state of daytime television and just quit. This might have been the response many would have chosen. Instead, she recognized this situation as an avenue to bring more positivity and growth into the world. Instead of succumbing to the darkness being perpetuated on television, she defined it as her opportunity to bring more light.

If the thesis for talk shows had been the tabloid format that Oprah helped to pioneer, and the antithesis became the trash-TV of Jerry Springer, Oprah's decision to keep the format and change the content created a new synthesis—a new standard for daytime television.

Finally, she told a new story—clearly, inspiringly, and frequently. Her talk-show guests gave people hope and inspiration. In addition to hosting the talk show, Oprah founded a magazine, created her own network, wrote her own television shows, acted, produced movies, and started a book club. Instead of walking away from an industry that seemed to use negativity and exploitation to get ratings, Oprah found more and more ways to act as if she was in control of the media.

Today she is an arbiter of popular culture, spirituality, social justice, health, and well-being, and she has uplifted millions of people in the process.

By practicing E+R=O, defining meaning and telling a powerful new story, Winfrey, like Lincoln, navigated change using the audacious strategy of acting as if. All it takes is one leader with a clear vision and the ability to articulate it to their followers. Claiming the meaning of events and maintaining the foresight to see the good in your experience even before it has become a reality, will, in fact, make it a reality.

If you are leading an organization through change, create the reality you want, even before it manifests. Claim the highest outcome, say it to everyone who will listen, and act as if this is already the case. Your optimism will be contagious. Watch as the entire team gets on board, and the reality you want arrives.

Exercises for Acting as If

- Write your ideal scenario for a current situation. If you found a magic lamp and the genie jumped out to grant you any wish, what would this situation look like? Write it in the present tense.
- Condense this scenario into a single statement of intention.
- Take an event you want to change and decide what ultimate outcome you want. Look at various responses. Which is most likely to get your outcome?
- Think of a negative condition happening now. How are you interpreting the situation? What

would be a more beneficial interpretation? Can you pivot your thinking?

- Evaluate how you talk to your team about your product, service, market position, or some aspect of your business. Can you tell a different story?
- How do you maintain control over your emotions? What can you do to shift your own attitude so that you act as if authentically?

7

Staying Constant amid Change

Everything will be okay in the end.
If it's not okay, it's not the end.
—JOHN LENNON

You now have five audacious strategies to navigate any change that comes your way. These strategies will make the difference between experiencing changes as catastrophes or catalysts. You no longer have an excuse to hide, play small, or curl up in a corner when change comes your way. Now you know exactly what to do. You can use any one of these strategies or combine them to be most effective.

Because you can't lead anyone where you haven't yet been, you must begin by becoming personally comfortable with change. The best strategy for this is to lean into it. In this option, take control of your relationship with change. Monitor how you think about change and constantly remind yourself that nothing good comes without change. Look back and think about what has changed in the past and remember that, even if it looked bleak in the moment, those changes propelled you forward.

Finally, you can learn to anticipate change. Nothing stays the same forever. Look around and ask, where do I see change coming? How might it appear? What would I do if things changed in this certain way? Be ready when it happens because you know that change is inevitable.

Depending on the situation, maybe your best, most audacious strategy is to defy the odds. There is probably a well-calculated, safe path for every situation, but sometimes that path isn't the most effective. First, reconnect with your purpose. Get clear on what, exactly, you want to accomplish and why. Next, look at your systems and resources. Take a comprehensive inventory of what you have and get to know what's *inside* your organization. After that, look at what is *outside* your organization. Who are your competitors? What are they doing? Could any of it relate to you?

Watch for tipping points—those small things that make a big difference. Finally, be proactive and anticipate situations and reactions. If everything seems right, you can defy the odds.

It could be that whatever change you're facing requires you to do the unexpected. If so, your top priority is to build trust within your team. Practice transparency, integrity, clarity, empathy, and inspiration. If your success depends on people following you in rapidly changing, stressful environments, take the time to get to know them, let them know who you are, and build a foundation of trust that allows them to be audacious followers. If you've invested in building trust, your team will follow you eagerly into the unexpected.

Sometimes, change requires you to know when to do nothing. Contrary to its title, this takes an abundance of knowledge and planning. To know when to do nothing, you not only need your team's trust, but you must also trust them implicitly. After evaluating all the options, decide that no action will improve the situation. Start by identifying your strengths. Take a personal and personnel inventory—of the character, traits, strengths, and talents of everyone you lead—and determine if they can hold in the face of challenge.

Remember, it can be to your advantage to lure the competitor into the cycle of escalating commitment, wearing themselves out fighting against your refusal to respond. You also must be willing to incur losses, even as you know you will ultimately prevail. Last, before you can successfully do nothing, you must have alternatives to do *something*, since the situation can change in an instant.

Finally, regardless of the change in front of you, you can act as if. The world is what you make of it. Remember the formula of E+R=O. For every event, choose your response, and therefore dictate the outcome. Once you've chosen a response, it's easy to intentionally define the overall meaning of a situation. This means taking control of communication momentum and telling the story you want to have remembered. Once you've told the new story, you have influenced your team to act as if the change is a springboard rather than an anchor.

Whichever of these five audacious strategies you use, either singularly or in combination, they will have the result of making you, your team, and your organization stronger and more resilient. When you are comfortable with change and learn to lead people through it, you don't need to worry about what is next on the horizon. You know you and your team can handle it, and you have steps ready for the next time change comes around.

When faced with a major change, everyone wants it to be delayed to five years from now. It would be nice to know what the outcome is and that everything turned out okay. Since people are fundamentally uncomfortable with changes, they want to get through them as quickly as possible and enjoy the peace on the other side. The journey is the audacious part, however, and these five steps will not only make the transition smoother but teach you how good you and your team really are.

Acknowledgments

I have been devoted to the study of history, spirituality, and leadership for most of my adult life. It is almost impossible to determine where, exactly, the ideas for this book started, since they are a conglomeration of my decades of study and experience. However, there are a few important people who stand out.

I want to begin by thanking my daughter, Kinsey Morley, for choosing to attend Penn State University and giving me a reason to travel through Gettysburg on a regular basis. Without these quarterly visits, I might not have fallen in love with the area.

I want to thank Steven B. Wiley and Angela Sontheimer for offering me the opportunity to join the faculty of the Lincoln Leadership Institute at Gettysburg. Without that offer, I wouldn't have ended up living in this historic and inspiring town.

I also want to thank my LLI colleague Joe Mieczkowski, a Licensed Battlefield Guide at the Gettysburg National Military Park. Joe's enthusiasm and encyclopedic knowledge of the battle have provided much food for thought throughout the writing of this book.

There are so many people to thank for supporting me in my leadership journey throughout the years. They include Kathy Hearn, Gregory Toole, Michelle Medrano, Steve Burton, Cynthia James, Ras Smith, Patty Luckenbach, and Roger Teel. These ministers and spiritual leaders have shaped and guided me as I struggled with profound life-changing issues.

I want to thank the congregation of Foothills Center for Spiritual Living in Evergreen, Colorado, for being the sounding board for so many of my thoughts and theories about emotional intelligence, leadership, and the Battle of Gettysburg.

I am grateful to my historical mentors and history professors over the years who taught me solid methodology and ways to apply history to the larger context of the human story. I especially appreciate Virginia Scharff, Paul Andrew Hutton, and Tom Noel.

I am so appreciative of all the nonprofit and for-profit organizations that have given me leadership roles in the past thirty years. Without the experiences at these organizations, I wouldn't have practiced and honed my leadership skills.

Finally, I want to thank my stepdaughter, Cleo Burton, for choosing a college in New York, which convinced her father to move east with me.

Last, but certainly not least, I want to thank my beloved husband, Steve Burton, for saying "yes." I couldn't take this journey without you, sweetheart.

About the Author

Dr. Judy Morley is a nationally recognized business speaker and coach whose primary topics include conscious business, purposeful leadership, and emotional intelligence. Her main focus is to help entrepreneurs and business owners lead purposefully, authentically, and audaciously.

Her years of experience vary from being an advertising agency owner to a college professor to an executive to an entrepreneur and restaurant chain owner. She is even an ordained minister. Each of these positions has given her great insight into helping people find their authentic style of leadership.

Dr. Morley holds a PhD in American History and a master's degree in Conscious Leadership, as well as being a certified Emotional Intelligence facilitator.

She is the author of more than a dozen essays and books, including *5 Spiritual Steps to Overcome Adversity: Use the Cosmic 2x4 to Hit a Home Run.* She has been featured in several documentaries, including *MPower: Empowering Women in Business and Beyond.*

Dr. Morley is on the faculty of the Lincoln Leadership Institute at Gettysburg and serves as the president of Intuitively Speaking, a leadership coaching firm located in Gettysburg, Pennsylvania.

She and her husband are the founders and owners of Tilford's Wood Fired Pizza, with locations in Colorado, Texas, and Pennsylvania, and the nascent concept SavorHood, an outdoor eatery park.

You can connect with Dr. Morley online at www.drjudymorley.net.

CPSIA information can be obtained
at www.ICGtesting.com
Printed in the USA
JSHW071720191222
35156JS00006B/156